Endorsements

Carolyn Thomas' first book, *War Dancer* has been superbly written! You can hear the wisdom that is only learned sitting at the feet of a loving Savior. You can feel the strength that is only gained battle after battle in spiritual warfare. And, you can feel the tender love that is genuine and deep, birthed in a heart committed to a call from God. No one will ever regret adding this ministering devotional to their library. Truly, it is a gift from God.

— Reverend Irma E. Gunnels

Amazing, touching, moving, these are just a few words to describe Carolyn Thomas' *War Dancer.* As a survivor I would have loved having this book when I was going through childhood sexual abuse. War Dancer speaks directly to the heart and spirit of the survivor, pouring in hope and love and light. It is not a must read, it's a must experience to anyone young or old who have experienced abuse.

— Talisha Story

LIFERESTOREDSA.ORG

WAR DANCER

A 40-DAY DEVOTIONAL FOR GIRLS WHO HAVE SUFFERED ABUSE.

CAROLYN A. THOMAS

Life Restored
San Antonio, Texas

War Dancer

Life Restored SA
14546 Brook Hollow #405
San Antonio, TX 78232

www.liferestoredsa.org

ISBN: 978-1-7330997-1-4

Printed in Canada

Cover Design & Typesetting
Stevie Griffin

About the Cover
The ballerina painting is representative of all the girls who are survivors of sexual exploitation. They are beautiful free spirits who have been shackled by adverse experiences that were forced upon them. We are blessed to watch them as they break through the pain and bondage of their pasts. With shackles broken, they dance uninhibited.

Dedication

To my beautiful daughters
Jasmine and Jannie,
My beautiful
Life Restored Girls,

And all the girls who never told.

War Dancer

"You are the God who sees me," for she said, "I have now seen the One who sees me."

GENESIS 16:13 NIV

When no one else is watching, I am. I'm always watching. I watch as you put away your sword and lower your shield. I watch as you relinquish your metal breast plate revealing the soft pastel chiffon and tulle garment beneath it. I am mesmerized as you pull off the helmet, allowing your hair to tumble to the nape of your neck. I am just as mesmerized as you wash away the war paint, allowing the innocence of your face to be illuminated. It is with such grace that you lower your body to the floor like a feather gently floating to its resting place. There, you remove the huge combat boots, revealing a pair of ballet slippers. Like a bird taking flight, you rise to your feet. It's then that I clearly see you. I can see that you, the mighty warrior, are a small, but powerful dancer. Dancing on all the negative words spoken to you, over you, and about you. You dance on the ill wishes of those who opposed you. You dance on the misguided notions of those who doubted your abilities as a warrior. You dance on the intentions of those who abused you. You dance on the soul ties that once bound you, holding you captive physically, emotionally, and spiritually. And it's the power of your dance that crushes all that is beneath your feet. You dance until they're no longer recognizable. And you dance. There is no weapon formed against you that will prosper. No words, no notions, no abuse, no binds. And so you dance until there is nothing beneath your feet. Nothing more than dust blowing in the wind.

Contents

Foreward i

Getting Started iii

A Note from the Author: v

DAY 1 An Invitation: Your Presence is Requested 1

DAY 2 My Gift to You 3

DAY 3 It's Not Your Fault 5

DAY 4 I Have Chosen You 7

DAY 5 The Places You've Been And… 9

DAY 6 He Calls Me His Beloved 11

DAY 7 Wiping the Slate Clean 13

DAY 8 Knowing the End from the Beginning 15

DAY 9 Letting Go 17

DAY 10 A Teaspoon Versus An Ocean 19

DAY 11 Revenge Isn't So Sweet After All 21

DAY 12 You Are Worthy 23

DAY 13 I Was There All The Time 25

DAY 14 You Are The One 27

DAY 15 When I Do What I Do 29

DAY 16 Blown Away 31

DAY 17 Taking A Stand 33

DAY 18 You're On The Wrong Plane 35

DAY 19 So You Think You're Not Good Enough 37

DAY 20 A Call To Forgive 39

HALFWAY BONUS – You Must Forgive! 41

DAY 21 Seeing Yourself Through the Eyes of God 45

DAY 22 Umoja: Better Together 47

DAY 23 Dinah 49

DAY 24 When Your 'Ride or Die' Don't Ride 51

DAY 25 Breaking the Cycle 53

DAY 26 Don't Count Me Out 55

DAY 27 Cast Into The Sea 57

DAY 28 When Life Gives You Crap 59

DAY 29 From Pit to Palace 61

DAY 30 Who Are Your People? 63

DAY 31 Casting Stones 65

DAY 32 A Call for Justice 67

DAY 33 Grenade 69

DAY 34 My Prodigal Daughter 71

DAY 35 What's Your Issue? 73

DAY 36 A New You 75

DAY 37 All The King's Horses 77

DAY 38 Battle Scars 79

DAY 39 I Have Redeemed You 81

DAY 40 The Company We Keep 83

A FINAL BONUS – Who Is This Jesus? 85

The Roman Road 87

Prayer Of Decision 88

What Now? 89

Acknowlegements 90

About the Author 91

Foreword

Through the many years of my ministry as a pastor, the Lord has blessed me in many wonderful ways. I have enjoyed countless days when I have been very aware of the sweetness of His love. But, along with those days, seasons also have come with painful turns. Sometimes these seasons have been the result of my own stubbornness and pride. Other times, the hardships have come without any warning. Yet, it is in these seasons when a person can start asking deep-heart questions about God, questions that may not always have an immediate answer.

Looking back, I can now see what I could not during those seasons of pain, that the Lord never forgot me and that He never stopped His work to redeem (save) me. I now can see that in the middle of my doubts and questions, and even when I didn't know if I could pray, He was present. One of the ways He has shown this to me is through the presence (the words and actions) of people that really care about me. Well, let it be said then, that this little book that you hold in your hands today represents a sure sign that God indeed loves you. For you see, Carolyn has poured out herself in prayer and in reflection to write this book, with you in mind. She is that person that has come your way to show you that God deeply loves you and that, even when you couldn't see it before, He has always been at work to redeem you. As the prophet declared long ago, "But now says the Lord, He who created you, He who formed you, 'Fear not, for I have redeemed you; I have called you by name, you are mine.'" (Isaiah 43:1).

Since I have known Carolyn, I've seen in her many of the qualities that make her the right person to write this book of reflections, just for you. Here I want to mention only two: honesty and clarity. The Gospel is the most important and transforming news anyone can hear. But, as with any news, the messenger does make a difference. The more urgent the news, the more we need a messenger that can be honest with us, so we can listen, and also be heard, during the hard parts of the conversation. The messenger also needs to speak with clarity, without complicating or watering-down the crucial news we desperately need. Well, you will soon be glad to know that Carolyn speaks honestly and with clarity. For Carolyn has endured a pain that few have known. But, she also has a gift to speak to that pain and tell of God's redeeming grace. And she won't make it difficult to understand! Carolyn is that friend that we all wish we knew a long time ago. One who knows how to speak of the one love that makes all things new.

The real worth of the Gospel is proven through the darkest and saddest night. And that is exactly the worth of what you now hold in your hands, a book to help you see the light of Christ's love, even in the darkest night. As the poet, Fyodor Dostoevsky put it long ago, "The darker the night, the brighter the stars. "

As you open the pages of this book, open your heart and receive its wisdom with hope and anticipation, as a sign of God's faithfulness and love for you.

To Him alone be the glory,

Víctor R. Martínez

Associate Pastor of Missions and Cultural Engagement at Redeemer Presbyterian Church

San Antonio, Texas

Getting Started

Before diving into this devotional, to help you receive all God has for you I suggest you pray this simple prayer, or construct your own prayer:

Hello God, it's me ________________

I have so many feelings, and I've experienced so many things, bad things. I really don't know what I believe, but I do believe you are real. I just don't know how to connect you being real with my life, the two seem worlds apart.

I'm told that you are loving and kind and that you control all things. So, when all the bad things were happening to me, where were you?

I'm committing to this devotional so I can understand. I believe there is more to this life than the misery I've experienced. I believe you created me for a reason. Please help me get to know you.

Amen.

A Note from the Author

The content of this 40-day devotional comes from two distinct voices. One from myself, as the author, and the other from 'The Father's heart'. The entries from myself, as the author, come with love and insight that God has given me for those who have been wounded and are hurting by the abuse of others. The entries from the 'The Father's heart', are from God himself through both His Word and the prompting of the Holy Spirit.

Trigger Warning

War Dancer is a devotional written for those who have suffered the trauma of sexual abuse. It is designed to be a mentor/mentee experience, but can also be used as a small Bible Study tool or even for individual study. Each of the 40 entries is followed by Points to Ponder and Questions that are meant to act as a springboard for further thought and discussion. We recognize that anything experienced by any of the five senses during a traumatic event can later manifest itself as a trigger. For this reason, when used as personal study, we recommend that you seek out a seasoned Christian who can help with any questions you might have. If you're uncomfortable answering any of the questions, don't feel pressured, you can always revisit them later if you choose to.

DAY 1

An Invitation: Your Presence Is Requested

"I have loved you with a love that has no end. So I am showing my love to you so that you will move toward me"

JEREMIAH 31:3B EASY

From the Father's Heart

I'M EXTENDING THIS INVITATION in hope that you would come away with me on a journey of adventure, intimacy, and love in its purest form. The love that I extend to you is far greater than physical love. You see, I am love, the lover of your soul, and you are my beloved. I long to be with you for eternity. There is nothing about you that I don't already know. I know the desires of your heart, your deepest thoughts, and your greatest fears. I know the innocence of your child-like spirit. I know the things that you wish no one knew, and still I love you with a love far greater than you can imagine. You are mine, and I will pursue you until you accept my hand and totally surrender your love to me.

I know you've felt so alone, but I've always been there with you. You are my beloved; I have never left you, nor could I ever forsake you. In your darkest hours, my heart broke for all you endured. That chapter of your life is finished. Your journey through these 40 days won't be perfect and that's okay. Just keep coming back because I love you, and I want you to know more about that love. You see, you don't have to earn my attention or my love, you've already got it, and although life will bring challenges, the best is yet to come.

For the next forty days, set aside thirty minutes each day, so that we can walk together hand in hand. Allow me to slow down your race toward tomorrow, so that you can take in the beauty of today. My beloved, come spend this time with me so that you can know me as one knows an intimate friend. You'll find that I've been beside you all along, pursuing you.

POINTS TO PONDER: AN INVITATION

Can you believe it? The God of the Bible, who created heaven and earth, is seeking a relationship with you. The incredible thing is that God knows everything about you—the good, the bad, and the ugly—and He still wants a relationship with you.

Relationships are all about give, take, and compromise. In the space below, describe what you would bring to the table in a relationship with God, versus what God brings to the table. After you've made your list consider who the real winner would be in the relationship.

____

____

____

____

STUDY QUESTIONS

1. How do you envision a relationship with God?
2. Have you ever experienced the love that God is inviting you to know?
3. God knows the things you wish no one knew about you. How does that make you feel?
4. What do you hope to gain by having a relationship with God?

DAY 2

My Gift to You

"Consider how the wild flowers grow. They do not labor or spin. Yet I tell you, not even Solomon in all his splendor was dressed like one of these."

LUKE 12:27A NIV

From the Father's Heart

WHEN YOU AWAKEN in the morning, look and listen for all the beauty around you. It's not there by accident; I created it for you. I strategically placed the sparrows outside your window. They sing the songs I wrote for you, serenading you. When will you stop to listen? Would you please slow down and take my hand? Let us walk together through the garden of life, rather than continuing your race toward tomorrow's superficial dream.

With fresh new eyes, look at the sunrise and discover its many colors. I painted those brilliant colors just for your pleasure. The flapping of butterfly wings, the hum of the bumblebee, and even the morning dew on the grass is the evidence of the great love I have for you.

Everything I created is my gift to you, but you are a gift to me. You are my crowning glory. When I created you, I did so with precision, and then I breathed life into you. From that moment, you sought to know the origin of that breath, and so you've been searching for me your entire life. Your childhood prayers were precious, the purity of your faith was unsurpassed, even by seasoned saints. That's the place I long to share with you- that place where I move mountains because of your faith.

POINTS TO PONDER: MY GIFT TO YOU

The beauty of God's creation is all around us. We often miss it because we busy ourselves with things of little importance. We obsess with rushing toward the next thing, and we don't stop to enjoy the present moment. Stop the madness! Wake up earlier than usual and experience the sunrise. Listen for the many sounds that hide in the quiet stillness of the morning.

In the springtime, walk barefoot feeling the morning dew on the grass. The beauty and wonder that's all around you is no accident caused by the random gases of a big bang. It is the entire earth declaring God's glory!

In the space below, list the beauty and wonder you see in nature that you may have missed before.

____

____

____

____

____

STUDY QUESTIONS

1. When you look around, what do you see that God has created just for you to admire?
2. Because we are created in the image of God, we possess His creative nature. How do you express that creativity?
3. In what ways do you think people search for God? How can you search for God? List ways you've searched for God in the past.

DAY 3

It's Not Your Fault

For I will restore health to you, and your wounds I will heal, declares the Lord, because they have called you an outcast.

JEREMIAH 30:17A ESV

From the Father's Heart

WHEN YOU SUFFER TRAUMA as a child, physical, emotional, or sexual abuse (or even the trauma of parents divorcing), you may feel like it's all your fault. As a child, you don't understand that children are not responsible for the actions of adults, and so you take responsibility for your own trauma. In taking on that responsibility, you believe you deserve the abuse you receive. The deeper message is that you're not worthy of real love, just it's counterfeit "abuse" masquerading as love. Nothing could be further from the truth. You are created in my image, and I am God, I am Love. And you are deserving of me.

That message of unworthiness is carried into your preteen, teen, and adult life. If it's never addressed, you go through life attracting and accepting the counterfeits, never experiencing real love. As a teen, when your boyfriend hits or slaps you, it's not foreign to you. Everyone who has ever claimed to love you has slapped you around or abused you in some way. You reach a point where you don't just accept it, you come to expect it.

The truth is, it's not your fault. You are not responsible for the actions of adults. You do not deserve abuse in any form. The most important truth of all: **you are worthy of real love!**

POINTS TO PONDER: IT'S NOT YOUR FAULT

Abusers are major manipulators. They have a way of twisting the truth and making you feel responsible for the abuse you've endured. They often use phrases like, 'I just get so angry because I love you so much', or 'if you wouldn't do xyz, I wouldn't lose control'. No matter what the abuse is, the abuser blames the victim. What's worse is the victim often accepts the blame.

In the space below tell of a time when you accepted responsibility for your own abuse.

____

____

____

____

____

STUDY QUESTIONS

1. Have you ever felt responsible for what has happened to you and why?
2. How does knowing you're not responsible give you freedom?
3. You are worthy because God, who created you in His own image says you are valuable. When the message of you not being good enough comes up, whose message will you believe and why?

DAY 4

I Have Chosen You

"The name of the Lord is a fortified tower;
the righteous run to it and are safe."
PROVERBS 18:10 NIV

From the Father's Heart

I HAVE CHOSEN YOU because, like myself, you bear the marks of many stripes, having been beaten down and abused by the world without cause, and then mocked for having been abused. Like you, I have known the agony of suffering. I've chosen you because of the great love I have for you, in spite of your weaknesses. I've chosen you even though when others look at you they see a fortified fortress. A fortress you've constructed so strong that a mighty army could not infiltrate it, but I see you. I see your extreme vulnerability. I see the misuse of your innocence and naivety, so I know why the fortress was necessary.

My child, maintaining such a fortress is all-consuming. Allow me to be your mighty fortress, your strong tower, where you can come and be safe (saved). I laid down my life for you. Protecting you is my delight.

Lay open your wounds before me. Allow me to bring healing that only I can bring. The fruit of your pain, once ripened, will bear the healing properties of compassion for others. The pain that was bitter and almost impossible to swallow will be sweeter than the sweetest nectar. The strength that's gained from your pain will be sought after and will bring healing to many.

POINTS TO PONDER: I HAVE CHOSEN YOU

Those of you who have suffered at the hands of others have a true connection to Christ. He, more than anyone else, understands the pain and the shaming that you've endured. He understands your need to put up that protective wall, making you less vulnerable. But He wants to break down that wall and enter into an intimate relationship with you.

STUDY QUESTIONS

1. What walls have you put up to keep others out?
2. Can you look at what you have suffered and see a correlation to what Christ suffered?
3. How does it make you feel knowing Christ has suffered and has a connection with your own suffering?

DAY 5

The Places You've Been and The Things You've Done

"Come to me, all you who are weary and burdened, and I will give you rest..."
MATTHEW 11:28 NIV

From the Father's Heart

I DO UNDERSTAND your fears and doubts. I fully understand your hesitation to trust. But your argument that 'I don't know the places you've been and the things you've done', just won't hold up. I know everything you've done and every experience you've ever had. I know so much more than that, I know the sentiments of your heart. I know the doubts you have about being able to live up to my expectations. It's the reason I've invited you on this journey, so you can get to know me and know my expectations.

I know you feel like you've been carrying the weight of the world on your shoulders. Naturally, when you're carrying extra weight it slows you down, and tires you out. If you don't lose the extra weight after a period of time it's no longer considered extra; it becomes a part of you and you just accept it. The same is true for the burdens others have placed on you. They're really not yours to bear, but you've accepted them and they're weighing you down and stealing your joy and peace. I want to relieve you of those burdens. Allow me to exchange my load for yours. Mine is so much lighter, and you'll find that whatever I ask you to do, I also enable you to do it. Until now you've not really lived. I want to give you life in such abundance you can't even imagine.

So yes, I know the places you've been and the things you've done. I also know the places you will go and the things you will do, and for that reason I choose you.

POINTS TO PONDER: THE PLACES YOU'VE BEEN...

You know for someone who has never had chocolate, it's hard to describe what a wonderful treat they are missing. That kinda sums up the abundant life in Christ. Until you experience it, you just don't get it. You may think your past experiences disqualify you, but they are the reasons more than anything that you should experience this life. God wants to relieve you of the heavy load you're carrying and replace it with a much lighter load. He'll even help you carry that load.

STUDY QUESTIONS

1. What burdens are you carrying that are not yours to bear?
2. What burdens are you carrying that are the result of your actions? Do you think God can give you rest from those burdens?
3. In Matthew 11, Jesus says for the burdened and weary people to come to Him for rest. He also says that He will give us a burden that is easy to bear. What burden do you think Jesus is offering to us?

DAY 6

He Calls Me His Beloved

My Beloved is mine and I his.

SONG OF SOLOMON 2:16A NIV

There are voices all around me
Shouting loud and shouting strong.
Voices, voices everywhere
From people that I know,
People who should love me
But love they never show.

They always find my weakest spot
And there they start to jab.
Blow after blow with all their might
'Til I can take no more.
Stopping when they're satisfied,
And I lay crumpled on the floor.

You're not so smart,
You're not so pretty.
Who do you think you are?
Then the words that I so dread,
"You'll never be nothing,
Like your no-good dad."

Sometimes I just want to scream
"Can anyone feel my pain?"
That's when I hear His voice so clear
"My child I hear your cry,
And though you feel so all alone
I've never left your side."

Still their voices are loud and strong,
But the words I no longer hear.
For there, you see, is another voice
Soft and gentle and oh so clear.
As He gently whispers in my ear

When He calls me His Beloved.

They say I'm too skinny
Too fat
Too dark
Too pale
He says I'm fearfully and wonderfully made
And He calls me His Beloved.

They tell me I'm no beauty queen,
He says I'm royalty.
They say I'm worthless,
He says I'm priceless
And gave His life for me
And He calls me His Beloved

So, though their words are vile and cruel
Why should they bother me?
When the very God of all creation
Died for me on Calvary.
His sweet, sweet voice drowns their loudest shouts
When He calls me His Beloved.

POINTS TO PONDER: HE CALLS ME HIS BELOVED

Our world can be awfully cruel, and, for many of us, the cruelty comes at the hands of those who should love and protect us. For those of us who fall into that category, God promises that when our mother and father forsake us, he will take us up. We are His beloved and he will never leave us or forsake us; that we can count on.

STUDY QUESTIONS

1. What do you think it means to be God's Beloved?
2. A good name is better than riches and favor is better than silver and gold. How would those who really know you describe your character?
3. It's very important that you clearly know who you are and your worth. List 3 things about your character that set you apart from others.

DAY 7

Wiping the Slate Clean

If we confess our sins, he is faithful and just to forgive us our sins, and to cleanse us from all unrighteousness.

I JOHN 1:9 KJV

HAVE YOU EVER LOOKED AT YOUR LIFE and thought, "What a mess"? I certainly have. Imagine your life as a huge chalkboard like those you'd find in an old-fashioned classroom. For every bad decision you made in life there would be an X. There would be an X for every lie you told. 'I'm too sick to go to school today', or 'no sir officer, I was not speeding'. Big fat X's! For every bad thing you've done. For every poor choice you've made. For every fight you've had, and for every time you've talked back to an adult, an X. I'm sure you get the picture that each of our chalk boards would be covered with X's.

But, it doesn't have to stay that way. Because God knows everything, He knew that we would make a mess of things, and He knew we'd never be able to clean that mess up ourselves. God loves us, even as a messy chalkboard full of X's, and so He sends Jesus with this giant eraser. All we must do is acknowledge that we can't fix ourselves and that we need Him. He then takes that giant eraser and erases every X. He doesn't stop there because there's always some stubborn residue, so He takes a giant damp sponge and wipes the slate clean!

That's good news, but it doesn't stop there. We are not perfect, so we mess up again and again. In no time, all of our boards would be filled with X's again. You see, our messes and X's are sins. Because God loves us so much, He's given us a remedy for sin. He doesn't want us to hide our sins or pretend they don't exist. He simply wants us to confess our sins, and He then forgives us and cleans our slates again. God's mercies are new every morning, which means that every day He has new compassion toward us to forgive us. How wonderful is that, exchanging our messes for His compassion and forgiveness!

POINTS TO PONDER: WIPING THE SLATE CLEAN

This clean state deal seems too good to be true, but it is true. God loves you beyond all comprehension. He wants to have a relationship with you. Take Him up on the offer.

STUDY QUESTIONS

1. Some sins are habits you've developed over time. Breaking habits are not easy, but the freedom you gain is worth the pain. What habits have you developed that may require help getting free of?
2. Sometimes the problem is the people we hang out with. Name your three best friends and tell what attracts you to them.
3. God knows when you're trying to do what's right and when you're choosing to do what's wrong. Never let the fear of future mistakes keep you from asking for forgiveness today. God's mercy is new every morning. This means when you mess up you don't have to remain a mess. What's stopping you from asking God to forgive you of your sins?

DAY 8

Knowing the End from the Beginning

"I make known the end from the beginning,
from ancient times, what is still to come."

ISAIAH 46:10A NIV

ATOMIC TRAIN was one of my family's favorite movies. There was plenty of action, and it kept us on the edge of our seats. We watched this movie time and time again, and it never got old. Even though we watched it many times and knew the ending, we watched with the same intensity as we did the first time.

That's how I make sense of God knowing the end- even from the beginning. He has done more than just read the last chapter of the book. He knows the exact sequence of every little detail of your life, and He has a plan to make everything work in your favor. Understanding that concept will help you make sense of your life.

When you're violated at a young age, there's a part of you that's stuck there. If you're violated repeatedly, anger builds, and you become a ticking time bomb. You're too afraid to tell anyone because the threats are scarier than the abuse, so the anger continues to build. Now you're a teen and that anger seems to have a mind of its own, exploding whenever it wishes. Fighting is your favorite pastime; you'll fight for any reason because it gives you a sense of control (although you're clearly out of control), and it makes you feel alive. It's gotten you in trouble more times than you care to remember. Everyone has always said you'd never amount to anything, and you start to think maybe they are right.

News Flash! Everyone is wrong. God says He has a plan for you, a good plan. A plan that will prosper you, give you hope and a future. He says that because He knows the end- even at the beginning. Never let your past define you. Never accept anything spoken about you or to you that contradicts what God says about you. No matter how dark this chapter of your life appears, God says you are the head and not the tail. Remember, He's not only read the book, but He is also the author and publisher of the book. He's not only seen the movie, but He's also the producer and director.

POINTS TO PONDER: KNOWING THE END

There are lots of twists and turns in our lives. So often, it seems that things are out of control, and they may very well be. While we may not be in control at every moment, we can be certain that all things are in God's control. While God does not orchestrate every moment and choice we make, he does have an end plan for us. His plans will cause us to prosper, are never designed to harm us, and His plans will give us hope and a future. It's clear that our lives are empty, but God will cause us to prosper. We are without hope, but, hope will flourish like wildflowers overtaking a field. And so we can look forward to a bright future, when once we couldn't imagine ourselves ever reaching adulthood.

STUDY QUESTIONS

1. If a snapshot was taken of your life right now, what would it look like to others?
2. God has promised to prosper you and give you hope and a future. Knowing this, use your greatest imagination and describe your life in ten years.
3. Every dream requires a plan and hard work to become a reality. List ways you can make your dream a reality.

DAY 9

Letting Go

"Forgetting what is behind and straining toward what is ahead, I press toward the goal to win the prize for which God has called me heavenward in Christ Jesus."

PHILLIPPIANS 3:13-14 NIV

YOUR FIRST EXPERIENCE sets the standard for every experience to follow. Wouldn't it be great if we all started out in an ideal family? We'd have a mom and dad who'd love each other and they would model what a healthy relationship looks like. The problem is that not many of us grew up in that ideal situation.

When abuse is part of your foundation, it becomes your norm. When abuse is modeled, you learn from it. You learn how to excuse it, you learn how to deny it, you even learn how to defend it.

When, as a child, you're sexually abused by what should be a trusted adult, it sets the stage for a lifetime of abuse. But, you don't have to play that part. God has plans for your life, plans that are good. Plans that will benefit you and give you hope and a future. But first, you've got to trust Him enough to let go.

Let go of the past hurts and the past disappointments. Let go of the idea that you're incomplete without a partner. Let go of your own insecurities. Let go of your Hollywood perception of love. Right now, you're holding on tightly with both hands to a toxic, unhealthy, abusive relationship. As you learn to let go, you'll find that God is preparing you to receive the blessings He has already made ready for you. It's only when you've let go that you can freely grasp what God has prepared for you, and only you.

POINTS TO PONDER: LETTING GO

When you fail to let go of hurts, betrayals and mistreatments, they keep you stuck in the past. Rather than filing them away, hoping you'll never need to deal with them again, you keep them front and center in your mind.

No new relationship is safe in the shadows of the old. You find yourself constantly reaching for a fire extinguisher to blow out a candle. Letting go of past relationships will allow you to relax and enjoy the blessings of new healthy relationships.

STUDY QUESTIONS

1. What are some practical steps we can take in letting go of old baggage that keeps us stuck in the past?
2. How can you choose not to let your past control you?
3. By holding so tightly to the thing that's in your past, you can't grasp the more excellent thing that God has designed for you alone. What are you holding on to so tightly that you should let go of?

DAY 10

A Teaspoon Versus An Ocean

"For God so loved the world, that he gave his only Son, that whoever believes in him should not perish but have eternal life."

JOHN 3:16 ESV

From the Father's Heart

THE AVERAGE LIFETIME IS 70 YEARS. When you're a teenager, 70 years seems like an eternity. The truth is, in the vast span of eternity, 70 years is like a teaspoon of water in the Pacific Ocean, the largest body of water on earth, with more than 60 million square miles of water. I'm asking you to surrender your teaspoon of water, and I, in turn, will give you the entire Pacific Ocean.

Surrendering your life seems hard, maybe even impossible, when you've been hurt and disappointed as much as you have. Until now, you've not known me. You've only known the counterfeit, whose purpose has been to exploit you for their own profit. I've asked you to come with me on this journey, so you can get to know me and the depth of love I have for you. When you know me in that intimate way, you will understand that surrendering comes with benefits that are far greater than anything you would ever give up. Because you are mine, I have lavished my love upon you. I have come so that you can live life more abundantly.

Surrender your teaspoon of water and I will give you the Pacific Ocean.

POINTS TO PONDER: A TEASPOON VERSUS AN OCEAN

She wants what she wants, and she wants it now. I'm talking about my two-year-old granddaughter, Peyton. Peyton knows nothing about delayed gratification, which is not accepting one cookie now, but waiting five minutes and getting three cookies. At 26 months, I don't expect her to know it, but when she's five and has a concept of time, I'll offer her the one cookie, but give her the option of waiting five minutes for three cookies. I want her to understand that waiting is not a bad thing, and that it has benefits. Too many adults have not learned that lesson. God offers us eternal life, and in all honesty, there is no trade off. What you give up is sin which leads to death, and what you gain is life everlasting.

STUDY QUESTIONS

1. God wants to give you so much more than you can imagine, but it requires you to trust Him. What stops you from trusting God?
2. Do you feel like becoming a Christian will stop you from having a fun and fulfilled life? Do you know any real Christians your age?
3. I challenge you to find a Bible-believing church in your area and attend a youth event. Once you've done that, go back and answer question #2 again.

DAY 11

Revenge Isn't So Sweet After All

"As a mother comforts her child, so will I comfort you..."

ISAIAH 66:13 NIV

TAMAR WAS A VERY BEAUTIFUL young woman. Her father, David, had many children, making her the product of a blended family. Among her siblings were Amnon, her half-brother, and Absalom, her full brother.

Tamar was so beautiful that Amnon, her half-brother, fell in love with her, so much so, that he couldn't think of anything but her. At the suggestion of a friend, Amnon pretended to be sick and requested that Tamar take care of him. It was a plot to get her alone. Tamar rejected all his advances. She tried to reason with her half-brother, even suggesting marriage, which in their culture would have been acceptable, but Amnon would not listen to reason. He raped Tamar.

After Amnon raped Tamar, he hated her to a greater degree than he had loved her. As Tamar grieved the loss of her innocence, Amnon harshly demanded that she 'get up and get out'. When Absalom found his sister distraught and crying uncontrollably over her state, he asked that she not tell their father, he would handle the matter.

The trauma of rape was more than Tamar could bear; she entered a state of depression. Even two years later, when Absalom had their half-brother killed, Tamar remained in her brother's house still in a state of depression. Absalom, now a murderer, went into hiding making him also a fugitive. It is said that revenge is sweet, but it never brings about healing. Forgiveness does.

POINTS TO PONDER: REVENGE ISN'T SO SWEET AFTER ALL

Tamar's story starts long before she is born, it starts with her father David. David was a great king, with so much power, but he could not control his lust for another man's wife. Because David didn't deal with the lust in his own life, that same spirit of lust can be seen in his son Amnon, as he rapes Tamar, his half-sister.

Chances are you've heard it said: "What happens in this house/family stays in this house/family." When we hide issues rather than deal with them, we give them time and space to incubate and grow into monstrous issues.

STUDY QUESTIONS

1. What secrets are in your family's closet that should be dealt with rather than remain hidden?
2. Have you ever felt abandoned by the people who should have protected you? Explain.
3. Are there people in your family that you need to forgive? If possible, write them a letter expressing how they have hurt you, and end the letter forgiving that person or persons.

DAY 12

You Are Worthy

"...we are children of God, and if children, then heirs-heirs of God and fellow heirs with Christ, provided we suffer with Him in order that we may also be glorified with Him"

ROMANS 8:16C-17 ESV

From the Father's Heart

IMAGINE FINDING OUT THAT you're not who you think you are, instead you find that your real father is royalty. All this time you've been living like a pauper when in reality you're a real live princess. Think about it. How much would your life change? How would this new status change the way you see and feel about yourself?

You've always felt so unsure of yourself, less than others. You've never felt good enough, or pretty enough or smart enough. That's because you didn't know your worth, and so you fell for the lies of the predator, the imposter. You looked at him and saw him through a faulty lense. You saw him from the seat of a pauper rather than the throne of a princess. You indulged him in the dance of social media. His seduction was cunning. He studied you long before you were even aware of his existence. He carefully chose you, knowing your worth, and knowing that you weren't aware of your worth. He knew you longed to belong, to be loved. He used your lack of knowledge against you.

I am here to redeem you. You are mine. I created you. I know you completely. I know when you sit down and when you stand up. I know your thoughts from afar. I have written you a love letter, it will help you understand who you are and reveal your true value and worth. What you know as the Bible is my love letter to you, and I'd love for you to read it sometime.

I am God, but not just God, I am your God! You are my daughter! That makes you royalty and worthy of eternal life... I am proud to call you mine.

POINTS TO PONDER: YOU ARE WORTHY

The life of a pauper is very different from that of a princess. As children of God, we have access to so many benefits. But if we don't know we're entitled we will never take possession of them. The Bible is a love letter from God written to us. It's full of promises that we never take advantage of because we don't know they exist.

STUDY QUESTIONS

1. What do you think makes a person worthy?
2. Now that you know you're worthy, you've got to get rid of that pauper's mentality that wants you to believe otherwise. List 3 things that God promises to those who belong to Him.

    1. ____

    2. ____

    3. ____

3. God has already chosen you. He's waiting for you to accept Him as being your God. What does God being "your God" mean to you?

DAY 13

I Was There All The Time

"I will never leave you nor forsake you."

HEBREWS 13:SB ESV

From the Father's Heart

THERE WERE SO MANY TIMES that you cried out and asked me to rescue you. You thought that I wasn't there or that I didn't hear you. Then you convinced yourself that I wasn't real because I didn't appear as you thought I should. But I was there, and I did hear you. It was me who saved you.

You've suffered at the hands of evil men and you've wondered why an all-knowing, all-seeing, all-powerful God would not pound his fist at their evil deeds and strike them down. What about your own deeds? They've not always been honorable; in fact, you've made some choices that have put you on the tottering edge of life. You've been in situations so close to death that your lashes would be singed. Each time, I've steadied your steps on life's slippery edge or pulled you back from the flames, but I've never taken away your free will to choose that path.

Free will is a gift I've given you, the freedom to choose your own path. It allows you to make your own choices, good or bad. Because I have given it to you, I will never take it from you. Just as you have chosen to do bad things, so have others, and because of this the world you live in is very broken. It's filled with people who are broken. They do what satisfies them in the moment, not considering the cost others will pay. Not even considering the cost they will pay.

Just remember, I will never leave you or forsake you.

POINTS TO PONDER: I WAS THERE ALL THE TIME

The Bible tells us that it's impossible to please God without faith. Faith is believing something even when we can't see it. That's why it's important that we not 'live in our feelings', we must live in what we know to be true.

We won't always feel the presence of God, but we can always know that He is with us, because He's promised to never leave us or forsake us. And we can be sure that He is for us, even when the entire world seems to be against us. Take comfort in knowing that you and God alone can defeat the entire world.

STUDY QUESTIONS

1. When have you felt the farthest away from God? What caused you to feel that distance?
2. Bad things do happen to good people, and it's God who gives the grace to use those bad situations in a positive way. Can you look back now and see how God protected you from a bad situation in your past?
3. Are you open to knowing someone who knows you completely, who loves you completely, and can heal even your deepest hurts?

DAY 14

You Are The One

"I am the good shepherd: the good shepherd giveth his life for the sheep."

JOHN 10:11 KJV

From the Father's Heart

THE FATHER IS MEANT TO BE the first authority figure in your life. A good father is one who loves unconditionally, protects, provides, and sacrifices. Because the family unit is so broken, you may have a negative impression of just what a father is meant to be, and that creates a problem with your perception of me, as God the Father. I'm intent on changing that perception.

I'm not the angry fed-up judge, who's keeping score of your every wrong turn, waiting to dole out punishment. On the contrary, I want you to think of my role as that of a kind, caring and loving shepherd, tending his flock of 100 sheep. If one sheep is missing, that shepherd leaves the 99 in search of that one lost sheep.

I'm the Good Shepherd and you are my sheep. I will always love, protect and provide for you. No sacrifice is too great to make for you. Right now, you are the one, my precious sheep that is lost. I've left the 99 sheep to search for you. This little devotional book that you now read is part of my leaving the 99 and coming after you. There are people I'm placing on your path, some you'll encounter only once or twice. Others may be assigned longer, and for a few, it will be a lifetime assignment. They are earthly angels I've deployed to guide you along the way, and finally get you home. Take to heart the contents of this devotional, as it softly whispers into your ear the truth of my unfailing love.

You are my precious lamb, young and naive, never recognizing that the one you've put your trust in is the cunning wolf dressed in sheep's clothing. Yes, it's going to take time for your perception of me to change, but I've got an eternity, and you're worth every invested minute.

POINTS TO PONDER: YOU ARE THE ONE

God is our Heavenly Father. He is the ultimate example of what a father should be. Our natural fathers make many mistakes because they are human, but we should never let that blur our vision of God, who is a perfect father. No matter how many times we mess up, our Heavenly Father lovingly awaits us and rejoices when we return.

STUDY QUESTIONS

1. When you think of God the Father, what do you envision? When you think of a shepherd, what do you envision? In what ways are they similar?
2. When thinking of your own father, what memories come up? How do those memories help or hurt your view of God the Father?
3. Have you made the ultimate decision to return home to God and accept Him as your Heavenly Father? Take this time to turn to page 88 and pray the prayer of decision right now.

DAY 15

When I Do What I Do

"For I do not do the good I want, but the evil I do not want is what I keep on doing."

ROMANS 7:19 ESV

How can I explain what I don't understand?
I wanna do good, plan to do good, gonna do good,
But when I do what I do, it's not the thing that I would
And certainly not the thing that I should.

I can handle the pain
From the physical blows.
But this inner war
I just can't control.

I know of its evil, its cunning deceit,
I know how it ends in total defeat.
But what I see when I examine this flesh that I'm in,
Is the illusion of pleasure, that comes from sin.

Hey…it smells good, it looks good,
It feels and it tastes good.
It shines, it glistens, it glitters, it glows,
But in the end, we find it's only fool's gold.

I'm no longer a slave to this flesh that I'm in.
By grace I am saved and destined to win.
It's not of my own, wretched one that I am,
But thanks be to God, I'm delivered from sin.

POINTS TO PONDER: WHEN I DO WHAT I DO

It's a relief knowing you're not the only one to have gone through a situation- that someone else has encountered the same or a similar situation and has survived. More than two-thousand years ago, Paul, a disciple of Jesus, found himself in the very situation we so often find ourselves in.

I wake up in the morning and declare it's going to be a good day! I'm gonna follow the rules, do what I'm supposed to do, and stay out of trouble. BUT, before I even realize it, the very things I said I would not do, I find myself doing.

STUDY QUESTIONS

1. In two to three sentences, tell of a time when you were determined to do the right thing but ended up doing the opposite.
2. The poem talks about an inner war. How does this inner war compare to peer pressure?
3. Isn't it great to know that when you lose that inner war or you give in to peer pressure, you can go back and visit Day Seven of this devotional and have your slate wiped clean? Like Paul, God knows our weaknesses and extends grace to us with every new day He gives to us. He knows all things and He knows when we strive to do what's right even when we fail. What's keeping you from asking Jesus to clean your slate?

DAY 16

Blown Away

"Get up, be baptized and wash your sins away, calling on his name."

ACTS 22:16B NIV

CARRIE UNDERWOOD'S HIT SONG *Blown Away* tells the tale of a young girl who knows the abuse of a mean drunken father. She takes shelter in the storm cellar as her drunken dad lies passed out on the couch. Outside storm clouds are rolling in, and a twister is developing. Her one prayer is, 'blow it away'.

Carrie's right, "there's not enough rain in Oklahoma to wash the sins out of that house." There is a remedy for this young girl's pain, but it's not in the rain or the hope of the house being demolished in the storm. It's not even in the possible death of the mean ole mister of a dad. Her hope lies in trusting a man who over two thousand years ago hung on a cross. Jesus, and Jesus alone, can wash the sin away. Not from that house, but from each of our lives. You see those tear soaked whiskey memories would not be blown away; they may even be intensified, souring her 'sweet revenge'.

There are two ways to overcome your past: first see a counselor. Invest in yourself by getting the help you need. Don't withhold anything from your counselor; lay everything on the table. Holding back is holding on to unnecessary pain.

Second, know your future. God has a plan and purpose for each of our lives. Find your purpose. Once you know your purpose, the thing you're called to do, do it with all your might.

POINTS TO PONDER: BLOWN AWAY

When you've been hurt you want revenge. The drive for revenge can make you both emotionally and physically sick. Even after revenge is achieved, its sense of satisfaction is short lived. Most importantly revenge is not God's way. Revenge will cause more pain and never bring about healing.

STUDY QUESTIONS

1. Describe the hurt that you're hanging onto, that drives you to seek revenge.
2. What do you dream of becoming in life? Does the dream line up with your purpose in life?
3. Think of a time when you've acted out of revenge. How did it play out, and did it quench the thirst of wanting to right the wrong?

DAY 17

Taking A Stand

"Let your light so shine before men, that they may see your good works, and glorify your Father which is in heaven."

MATTHEW 5:16 KJV

INNOCENT PEOPLE SUFFERING at the hands of others is nothing new. History is peppered with suffering since time began, usually by one group trying to dominate another. It's hard to imagine that between 1941 and 1945 more than six million people were systematically murdered simply because they were Jewish. It was one man who ordered the extinction of millions, while the world turned its head and pretended not to see. What would your response have been had you lived during the time of the Holocaust? Would it have been easy to turn your head and look the other way? After all, it would not have been your battle; you would have had problems of your own. So, I'll ask again: What would your response have been?

When you've been mistreated, misused, and abused, it pushes you in one direction or the other. You can become angry and bitter. You may even find yourself perpetrating the same offense you suffered. Or you can become compassionate toward those who suffer abuse. Often what was your misery becomes your ministry.

In today's culture there are many opportunities to stand against injustice. So, what have you stood against? You've secretly prayed to be rescued. Now that you're free, have you helped anyone else get free? You're not called to save the world; that's God's job, but you are called to make a difference in the small piece of the world that you occupy.

POINTS TO PONDER: TAKING A STAND

Hitler was a bully. The world is full of bullies. How do you respond to them? Do you blend into the background and try not to make waves? Or do you speak up and take a stand against the evil that exists? Edmund

Burke once said, "Evil flourishes when good men do nothing." Are you willing to do something? Will you take a stand?

STUDY QUESTIONS

1. There is so much injustice in our world today. What are you willing to take a stand for, or against?
2. Tell of a time when you stood up for the underdog. What were the results?
3. Tell of a time when you needed an ally, and no one came to your defense.
4. What has been the source of misery in your life that can become your ministry?

DAY 18

You're on the Wrong Plane

"If I say to the wicked, 'You shall surely die,' and you give him no warning, nor speak to warn the wicked from his wicked way, in order to save his life, that wicked person shall die for his iniquity, but his blood I will require at your hand."

EZEKIEL 3:18 ESV

IT'S BEEN A WHILE since I've watched the movie *Home Alone 2: Lost in New York*, with Kevin McCallister, played by Macaulay Culkin. I recall the entire family being on a flight to sunny Florida to escape the harsh winter of Chicago. That is, all except the youngest son, Kevin, who through a series of bumbled mishaps, finds himself separated and on a plane bound for New York. It's always mystified me that we were to believe that a person could travel from Chicago to New York and never realize they're on the wrong plane. Surely it would have come up in conversation, or even mentioned by a flight attendant, but Kevin only realizes the mistake upon arrival to New York.

How long do we travel in life without a clear vision of where we're headed? It's easy to get caught up in our day to day meaningless routine. The glam and glitter distracts us from what is real and what is important. I wonder how many warning signs we miss. I wonder how often the truth is made available to us, but because it doesn't coincide with our Hollywood-induced ideas, we toss it aside. What is the truth? The truth is, unless you accept Jesus and make Him your Savior, you're headed in a direction you don't want to go.

How often have you heard the 'Gospel', the good news of Jesus Christ? It's the message throughout this book. How often have you heard or read the message of God's love for you? It's God pursuing you. My job is to sound the alarm and warn you to get off the plane whose final destination is Hell.

I must put aside my desire to be liked and accepted by you, and warn you that you're on the wrong plane. What kind of person am I when I fail to warn you? How do you feel about me, when you end up where you don't want to be, and find that I knew the truth and could have, but didn't warn you?

POINTS TO PONDER: YOU'RE ON THE WRONG PLANE

We would quickly pull someone back from the path of an oncoming vehicle, even if it were someone we didn't know. If we didn't, and that person was hurt or killed, we'd feel awful. When we see others living in a way that we know will bring about death, we should feel the same urgency as when that person is in the path of an oncoming vehicle.

STUDY QUESTIONS

1. Tell of a time when you saw someone in danger but didn't speak up. Why did you choose to be silent?
2. Death is like a bridge that gets you from here to your final destination: Heaven or Hell. If you had to cross that bridge today, where would it take you?
3. Are you receptive to the opinions of others or do you surround yourself with people who always agree with you? How do you respond when others disagree with you and voice their thoughts and opinions?

DAY 19

So, You Think You're Not Good Enough

"I came not to call the righteous, but the sinner to repentance."

LUKE 5:32 KJV

From the Father's Heart

IT CAN BE EASY to feel like you're not good enough. Often, it's the message you get from some Christians. Well, it's true and it's false. True, because you could never be good enough on your own, no matter how hard you try, no matter how long you live. False, because accepting my son Jesus makes you good enough. You see, when you accept Jesus in your life, He takes all your sins and exchanges them with His righteousness, making you good enough. You become complete in Him. In fact, that's why you are perfect to be used by me, even though you make mistakes. You are covered by my grace. I have never been fond of the outwardly self-righteous type, always publicly performing good deeds to be seen and praised by others. Those aren't the people I use. Actually, I have no use for them, but you are my chosen one.

Look in the Bible and you'll find that I'm drawn to those who are broken and bruised. I'm notorious for using 'shady' people. Remember Noah, the ark builder? He was once a drunkard! David, the 'man after my own heart' was previously a murderer and adulterer. Rahab, who in her past was a prostitute, is not only part of my heritage but a very important part. No matter what one's condition in life is, when there's a true encounter with me, that condition changes for the better. Their conditions become a thing of their past as they are made "new" in me. Take a closer look at those who were used throughout the Bible, and you'll never find a perfect person other than my son, Jesus.

If you'll allow me, I will take the brokenness of your life, pour in my all-sufficient grace and create a brand new you who will be a testament of healing and wholeness.

POINTS TO PONDER: SO, YOU THINK YOU'RE NOT GOOD ENOUGH

God created you. He fashioned you perfectly, just the way He wanted you. I imagine as with all his creations, He looks at you, steps back, takes a second look and says, "she's very good". When you say you're not good enough, you contradict what God says, and His words are weightier than yours.

STUDY QUESTIONS

1. What do David, Noah, and Rahab have in common?
2. Do you think any of these people could have cleansed themselves from the messes they were in? Could they be good enough to have a relationship with God?
3. What about you? Are you good enough to earn God's love and acceptance and have a relationship with Him? Why or why not?
4. It's a fact that Jesus died on the cross for your sins, making you 'good enough'. So, what's really keeping you from having a relationship with Him?

DAY 20

A Call to Forgive

"...and forgive us our sins, as we have forgiven those who sin against us."
MATTHEW 6:12 NLT

Jesus said, "Father forgive them, They don't know what they are doing."
LUKE 23:34A ERV

WHEN IT COMES TO FORGIVENESS, maybe you're like I was. I used to think forgiveness was for the weak, those who were push-overs who couldn't or wouldn't stand up for themselves. I thought that because I didn't understand forgiveness. I thought to forgive was to minimize the offense. I thought it would be like saying, "Oh, no big deal, it doesn't really matter", when yes, it is a big deal, and it does matter. I didn't understand that forgiveness was for me, not the other person. I have since learned that it takes a strong person to forgive. I've learned that when I forgive, I am free of the weight and burden of the offense and then the healing can begin.

Often when you've been violated, the perpetrator moves on and you are left stuck in a time warp reliving the abuse over and over. It's PTSD at its worst. Forgiveness is not likely when you're amid the abuse, and PTSD keeps you in the midst of the abuse. This puts you on an emotional rollercoaster. You bounce from one emotion to another repeatedly. It's denial, anger, bargaining, depression, and acceptance. The five stages of grief and loss, because you have suffered a loss.

If you were to break your leg, you'd go to the ER without hesitation. We should see emotional breaks in the same way. We'd never attempt to reset the broken bone ourselves and stabilize it until it's healed. When we're emotionally broken, we often try to self-medicate with alcohol, drugs, and other vices to numb the pain. This not only prolongs the pain, but can also create addictions.

Be kind to yourself. Just as you would seek an orthopedic specialist for a bone with multiple breaks, seek out a trauma informed therapist who can assist with the emotional trauma, and can help facilitate your healing.

POINTS TO PONDER: A CALL TO FORGIVE

Forgiveness is a necessary step in the healing process. If we harbor unforgiveness in our heart toward even the most vile perpetrator, it keeps us angry. Unresolved anger brings bitterness and sickness, and can even shorten your life expectancy. Forgiveness really is for you.

STUDY QUESTIONS

1. Who have you not been able to forgive? Why?
2. Feelings like anger, rage, and hate are self destructive, and the general wear and tear they put on your body can cause heart disease and so much more. When you think of the person that you haven't forgiven, what feelings rise up in you? Is it anger, rage, hate?
3. No one would willingly give their abuser power to abuse them, yet when you hold on to anger, hate and rage, that's exactly what you do. You give your abuser power to wreak havoc with your health and well being. List three things you can do to take your control back:
    1. ______________________________
    2. ______________________________
    3. ______________________________

HALFWAY BONUS

You Must Forgive!

"Jesus said, "Father forgive them, They don't know what they are doing."

LUKE 23:34A ERV

Congratulations you've reached the halfway mark of this book. If you're going to finish successfully you must forgive, so here's a small part of my story as a bonus:

AT THE AGE OF 14 my daughter was trafficked. At the time I didn't know what that meant. It was very difficult to learn that she had been held by a man in his thirties and sold to other men for sex. I was angry at this man, and I was angry at God!

I had two girls, and I was raising them to love God as I had been raised. I was doing things God's way. Why did God allow this awful thing to happen to my child? I never met her trafficker, but I hated him. For the first seven or eight months I didn't go to sleep before tears would stream down my face and pool in my ears. I hated this man that I had never seen. I had no face to attach the hate to, still I would never forgive him!

He had stolen my little girl, my 14-year-old who loved all things Disney. My girl who always wanted to sit on my lap, or hold hands as we walked through the mall. My girl who loved old black and white romantic movies, my girl who read all the Harry Potter books in record time, no matter how many pages they were. He had stolen her, and the girl she'd been replaced with was a girl I didn't know. She was a girl I didn't like. I would never forgive him!

I knew that he had probably moved on with his life, but we were stuck. I wanted this predator to suffer as he'd made my daughter suffer, as he made me suffer, as he made my entire family suffer. My daughter cried all the time, my oldest daughter spent less and less time at home, I developed stomach issues, my hair began to fall out and I didn't get much sleep. He had to suffer, and so I would fantasize about torturing this faceless predator. I didn't want to kill him, I just wanted him to suffer. I fantasized about shooting out both of his knee caps, so when God began to talk to me about forgiving him, I dismissed the thoughts as demonic. When God made it clear that I was to pray for his salvation and the salvation of other predators, I wanted to deny it was God speaking, but let's face it, only God would ask you to pray for your enemies. There was no denying it; God was asking me to do the impossible.

The truth is my life at that time was miserable. All I could think of was the awfulness of what happened. My daughter was constantly experiencing triggers that would send her back in time so she was stuck. It seemed the only one not stuck was the predator who was moving forward with his life. Once I understood that, I understood the need for forgiveness. But God asking me to forgive this faceless man was still asking me to do the impossible.

Was it impossible? It sure felt like it, but then I got this picture in my head of Jesus hanging on an old wooden cross. Jesus, the only person who was totally and completely perfect, without sin, hanging there between two criminals. He was paying the price for sins He never committed. Right there amid His suffering, He stopped to pray. My prayer would have been, God make them pay, make them suffer. But not Jesus, His prayer was: "Father forgive them, they don't know what they're doing." If Jesus, who is our ultimate example could forgive, then so could I.

Once I purposed to forgive, nothing changed immediately. There were no unicorns or rainbows, I didn't just forget all that happened. My family wasn't miraculously healed, but things did begin to change. A slow but consistent change. I can't tell you when the process was complete, but I can tell you that I'm no longer plagued with that burden of hate that was stealing my peace, my joy and my health. If you are to put your past behind you and move forward, you must forgive!

THE FORGIVENESS PROJECT

Forgiving is not easy, but unforgiveness is even harder. It's hard on your relationships with others. It's hard on your emotions. It's hard on your body, and it's hard on your mental and physical health. Write a letter of forgiveness to that person you struggle to forgive. It can be one page or

20 pages. Empty yourself of all the hate and rage and anger you have for that person. Your letter may take a day to write, or it may take a month, but get it all out. Once your letter is finished, sit with it for a day or two, read it again, making sure you haven't left anything out. Then, when you are ready, find a safe and quiet place and talk to God. Present the letter to Him. Cry, scream, do whatever you feel as you read each page aloud to God. Remain there in His presence until you feel a release. Once you feel that release, begin tearing the letter into tiny bits and pieces, so tiny that it could never be reconstructed again. Then dispose of it, not in one place but in several places. Celebrate your freedom!

For I know the **PLANS**
I have for ***YOU***,
Declares the **LORD**,
Plans to ***PROSPER*** YOU
And not to Harm you,
PLANS to give you ***HOPE***
And a **FUTURE.**

Jeremiah 29:11

DAY 21

Seeing Yourself through the Eyes of God

"For we are His workmanship, [His own master work, a work of art], created in Christ Jesus…"

EPHESIANS 2:10A AMP

"YOU IS KIND, YOU IS SMART, YOU IS IMPORTANT." It's so important that you know your worth. Important enough that God will cause the least expected person to intersect your life and give you the message. In the movie *The Help*, 'baby girl' didn't receive the affirmations and inspiration from her mother, but she would get what she needed by other means. The maid Aibileen Clark, played by Viola Davis, recognizes the lack of love, attention and self-worth given to 'baby girl' and instinctively speaks into the child's life.

God as our Father knows that we His children need to know our self-worth. He's given us the Bible, which is His love letter to us, but He knows we don't always read it, and so He dispatches earthly angels to speak into our lives. Those angels may be teachers, neighbors, mentors or just someone who sees great potential in you. This devotional serves as an angel, reminding you of God's word that says, "you are His workmanship, His masterpiece, His work of art".

God wants you to know how He feels about you. He wants you to know that you are beautiful and wonderfully made (Psalms 139:14). He wants you to know that He loves you so much. He wants you to know that you are so important to Him that He knows even the number of hairs on your head (Matthew 10:30). He wants you to know that He saves each one of your tears and He keeps them in a bottle (Psalms 56:8). God says you belong to Him (Isaiah 43:10). God says that you are victorious (1 Corinthians 15:57).

God calls you His beloved (Song of Songs 6:3), He says so many wonderful things to you and about you. You really should read that love letter and find out for yourself.

POINTS TO PONDER: SEEING YOURSELF IN GOD'S EYES

How do I love thee? Let me count the ways.

I love thee to the depth and breadth and height

My soul can reach,

STOPPPP!

Because as lovely as the words of Elizabeth Barrett Browning's sonnet is, It's a love that's incomplete.

God is love, so if He's not in the equation,

You're stuck with a problem, and never a solution.

STUDY QUESTIONS

1. Words are simply tools. They can build you up or tear you down. Think about the words that have been used to tear you down. How do they compare with what God says about you?
2. Who are the people speaking positive, affirming words into your life? Are you in return speaking positive, affirming words into the life of someone else?
3. God has so many positive and lovely things to say about you. Find three people and share some of God's positivity with them.

DAY 22

Umoja: Better Together

"Though one may be overpowered by another, two can withstand him. And a threefold cord is not quickly broken."

ECCLESIASTES 4:12 NLV

THERE ARE MANY CULTURES around the world where women have little or no rights; they are merely the property of men. Samburu, Kenya, is such a place. Women are oppressed in many ways. Girls are subjected to genital mutilation. Twelve-year-old girls can be forced to marry men old enough to be their grandfathers. Rape there is a common occurrence with no consequences.

One woman, Rebecca Lolosoli, took a stand against the injustice that she and other women were subjected to. In 1990, Rebecca established Umoja, a women only village. The village is built by women and run by women. Umoja is not just surviving, it's thriving.

It's easy to think we're so far removed from that type of bondage, but are we? Date rape is off the charts, and rarely reported. Girls who suffer sexual, physical and emotional abuse from "boyfriends" are becoming younger and younger. And sex trafficking pre-teen and teenage girls is the fastest growing crime in the world, and the US leads the way. We're not so far removed.

When Rebecca established her village she named it Umoja, which means unity. Unity- it's what we are missing in our culture. So often I hear young women say, "I don't like other females" or "I don't get along with other females". It's as if other females are some crazed species rather than just another version of themselves.

Ladies, we've got to change our mindset. We've got to become like the women of Umoja. We must be our sister's keeper! We must cover each other, protect each other and look out for each other. Give your sister a heads up when you hear she's in danger. We really are better together!

POINTS TO PONDER: UMOJA: BETTER TOGETHER

What an awful sight to see two girls fighting over a boy. There he is with the swollen head waiting to see which girl will prevail, but really, is he a prize? This guy who watches two girls kick, scream, and pull hair, is he really the one they want? If both girls knew their worth- the inherent worth that God has given them- they would understand that this boy is undeserving of either of them, and they'd both walk away together, refusing to play his game.

STUDY QUESTIONS

1. We really do teach others how to treat us by how we love ourselves. When you look in the mirror, describe the person you see. What do you love about this person? How do you express that self-love?
2. On *National Geographics* and *Animal Planet* there's usually a scene of a big strong powerful animal chasing a herd of less powerful animals. The chase continues until the weakest in the herd, which is usually the youngest in the herd, just can't keep up. It falls behind and is separated. This is the animal that becomes dinner. What do you think would happen if the herd decided not to run, but together stand their ground?
3. Here is the opening verse for today's devotional, what do you think it means? Rewrite it using your own words:
   A person standing alone can be attacked and defeated, but two can stand back-to-back and conquer. Three are even better, for a triple-braided cord is not easily broken.

DAY 23

Dinah

"In the same way, you who are younger must accept the authority of the elders."

1 PETER 5:5 NLT

From the Father's Heart

DINAH WAS THE TEENAGE DAUGHTER of Jacob and Leah, growing up in a house with older brothers. Dinah was a lot like you; she was beautiful, adventurous, and curious about the world and the people of other cultures. Much like you, it was her curiosity that got her into trouble. She wanted to know what life was like for those girls and women of other cultures and so, she ventured beyond the protected land of her father. As Dinah innocently wandered about the unfamiliar land, she caught the eye of Shechem, who was the son of Hamor, the ruler of the unfamiliar land. Shechem saw Dinah, he took her, and he raped her. Shechem realized that he loved Dinah, so he said to his father, "Get me this girl to take as my wife."

When Jacob heard that his daughter, Dinah, had been raped, he decided to wait until his sons returned home from working in the fields before taking any action. However, the raping of Dinah was so horrific that the news could not be contained, and so Dinah's brothers got the news while in the fields. The two brothers devised a scheme to get revenge on their neighbors by deceiving them. The scheme resulted in the death of every man in Hamor's village, but it came with a price. Hamor's village and all the surrounding villages banded together and instantly became Jacob's enemy. This not only put Jacob at risk to be killed, but his entire family and even his servants. Dinah's impulse to go beyond the protected borders put the entire community at risk.

POINTS TO PONDER: DINAH

It can be hard to see the big picture from where you are. Who would have thought that a virus that originated in China would bring about a world-wide pandemic? We are all connected! When we make choices and decisions it not only affects us, but it affects those that are connected to us. The next time you are tempted to step outside the boundaries, think of others that may be affected.

STUDY QUESTIONS

1. Borders, boundaries, and rules are put in place to protect us. How did Dinah's disobedience put her, her family, and her community at risk? Tell of a time when your choices or actions put others at risk?
2. We all need the protection of guidance and wise counsel, but it's often found outside of the flawed mom and dad authority figures we start out with. Who has God placed in your life that you can turn to for this wise counsel?
3. Dinah was 14 or 15 years old at the time of the encounter, the age when teens are seeking independence from their parents and also a time when teens need the wisdom of parents. How do you balance becoming independent and seeking the wisdom of those who God has placed in authority over you?

DAY 24

When your 'Ride or Die' don't Ride

"The third time he said to him, 'Simon son of John, do you love me?' Peter was hurt because Jesus asked him the third time, 'Do you love me?' He said, 'Lord, you know all things; you know that I love you.' Jesus said, 'Feed my sheep.'"

JOHN 21:17 NIV

ACCORDING TO URBAN DICTIONARY, the term 'Ride or Die' originated as a biker's term meaning that in the event you could not ride, you'd rather die. In today's culture it's any person, homeboy, homegirl, spouse, or BFF that will ride out any problem with you, or die in the attempt.

People will often announce themselves as your ride or die. Usually when the announcement is made, there's no ride or die situation. They are sincere and do mean well, but when the rubber hits the road and they are put to the test, they fail. Even Jesus had a ride or die. It was Peter. Peter loved Jesus, and upon learning of Jesus's approaching death, Peter declares that he would die with Jesus rather than disown him. Jesus tells Peter that before the rooster would crow, he would disown him three times. And it happened just as Jesus said.

Jesus didn't hold it against Peter. He knew Peter loved him. There are so many friends that say they've got our backs, but eventually they will fail us. While friends are essential in life and may very well have our best interest at heart, we can not be saved by others who are just as flawed as we are. Only God is perfectly faithful. We must put our hope and trust in Jesus, and allow him to have our backs and be our ride or die.

POINTS TO PONDER: WHEN YOUR 'RIDE OR DIE' DON'T RIDE

Does it surprise you to know that Jesus had a ride or die friend? Are you surprised that even Jesus was let down by his ride or die? We should never put all our hope in others who are just another version of ourselves. Although we look for people who will encourage and support us, our hope and trust must be in God. And we must realize there are some roads we must travel with God alone.

STUDY QUESTIONS

1. Who are the people you consider to be your ride or die friends? Why have they earned that title?
2. Have you ever been disappointed or let down by those people?
3. Have you ever disappointed or let someone down who you really wanted to be there for? How did you feel being the source of their disappointment?

DAY 25

Breaking the Cycle

"He heals the brokenhearted and binds up their wounds."

PSALMS 147:3 NIV

"I lay the sins of the parents upon their children and grandchildren; the entire family is affected- even children in the third and fourth generations."

EXODUS 34:7B NLT

From the Father's Heart

I KNOW THAT YOU LIVE IN A BROKEN WORLD and were born to broken parents, who were also born to broken people. It's a cycle, one that you have the power to break. Think of it like diabetes; your parents have it, their parents had it and, likely, you will have it and pass it on, unless you break the cycle.

If you have a family history of diabetes, you can prevent it by being very intentional and making changes. Not a one-time change, but a change in lifestyle. It won't come overnight; it requires work and commitment. Breaking the cycle of diabetes can be achieved by eating healthier, being physically active, and by reaching and maintaining a healthy weight.

Breaking the cycle of abuse requires work and commitment as well. It can be achieved by recognizing the abuse in your family's history. Own it! Don't sugar coat it or pretend it didn't happen. Be vigilant. Be proactive. Pulling up a seedling is much easier than digging out a mighty oak. Last, but certainly not least, you must reach and maintain a healthy self-image. It's easy to have a poor self-image when you've lived with abuse. Whether it's physical, emotional, or sexual, all abuse sends the message that you're not good enough. That you somehow deserved the abuse. Of course, that's a lie the perpetrator tells rather than taking responsibility for his or her own actions.

The best way to dismiss a lie is by knowing the truth. Forget every negative thing you've ever been told, and meditate on what God says about you. He has this plan for your life that's going to produce the best you imaginable! It starts with you breaking free of negative cycles, and trailblazing a new path of success.

POINTS TO PONDER: BREAKING THE CYCLE

Cycles can be hard to recognize. Because they've been with you so long, they've become your norm. It takes being very intentional to recognize that you're caught up in a cycle. There are many family cycles: alcoholism, teen pregnancy, drug addiction, incarceration, and so many more. Take a really good look at your family tree, both sides if possible. If it's possible, ask your parents about their life as a child. What were some of their challenges? Ask them about their parents and grandparents. Take notes if you can, and jot down all the similarities. In what way is your mom like her parents? In what way is your dad like his parents? Can you see a pattern? Now the big question: in what ways are you like them?

STUDY QUESTIONS

1. What patterns can you see in your family tree?
2. Name a cycle that you've already begun in your own life (i.e., cheating on tests, lying to parents, in and out of detention). What steps can you take to break that cycle?
3. Name a cycle that you'd like to be the first in your family to begin (i.e., first to graduate high school, first to go to college, first to purchase a home).

DAY 26

Don't Count Me Out

"This vision is for a future time. It describes the end,
and it will be fulfilled. If it seems slow in coming,
wait patiently, for it will surely take place."
HABAKKUK 2:3 NLT

THERE'S THIS STORY IN THE BIBLE about a kid named David. David was the youngest of eight boys. He was somewhat of a misfit in his family. His brothers were strong, tough, skilled warriors. David was rather scrawny, so his dad gave him the job of tending the sheep. Shepherding was not a sought-after job, and as in David's case, it usually came by default.

One day a prophet shows up at David's house and tells Jesse, his dad, that God has chosen one of his sons to be King. Just the thought of one of his sons being king made Jesse proud. The prophet had special instructions, so he knew how to determine which son would be King. Seven sons lined up, and the prophet examined them, but none were to be King.

The prophet then says to Jesse, "God has not chosen any of these; surely you must have another son." Jesse laughed, "yes, but he's just a scrawny kid who keeps the sheep. There's no way he could ever be King." "Bring him", insisted the prophet, and it was determined that God had chosen David to be the King.

How often have people judged you based on what they see, rather than who you're called to be. Don't be swayed by the perceptions and opinions others may have of you. The boy in our story is the same David who later defeated the giant Goliath. You are the modern-day David, capable of conquering any Goliath that comes your way.

POINTS TO PONDER: DON'T COUNT ME OUT

We can so easily count others out, just as we've been counted out, based on what people believe about us, and what they see. For a time, Joanne Rowling was jobless. She and her baby girl lived on welfare and were counted out by many. The book she had written, that would have a great appeal to boys, was rejected 12 times, simply because she was a female author. When her book, *Harry Potter and the Philosopher's Stone*, was finally published under the name J.K. Rowling, it was an overwhelming success. Joanne Rowling was counted out by many in her twenties, but today, she's made it to the top and is known world-wide. She is one of the most successful authors in the world.

Ignore those who count you out. No matter what it looks like right now, no matter how many rejection notices you receive, never give up and never give in. Remember, haters are gonna hate, but in the end, you win!

STUDY QUESTIONS

1. David was counted out because of his youth; Joanne was counted out because of her gender. For what reasons have people counted you out?
2. How does your family see you? As a skilled warrior or a weakling? How does that compare to how God sees you?
3. Although David was destined to be King and Joanne was a gifted writer, both had to work hard to realize their destinies. How can you begin working now in preparation for your destiny?

DAY 27

Cast Into The Sea

"...you will tread our sins underfoot and hurl all our iniquities into the depths of the sea."

MICAH 7:19B NIV

From the Father's Heart

THE DEEPEST SEA IS THE CARIBBEAN. It's 7,686 meters deep. Now imagine all your sins being thrown deep into the sea. That's more than 4 miles. Four miles into the depth of the vast sea, that's where I've thrown your sins. When you confess your sins to me, you get a complete 'Do over'. I not only forgive you, but I cleanse you as well, so that the stain of your sin is made whiter than snow. Because of my great love for you, I have compassion on you. It is my delight to offer you mercy rather than judgement, and that mercy is renewed every day. Not only do I cast your sins into the sea, but I choose to remember them no more. I will never bring up those sins again. They will never be thrown in your face or used to judge, shame or discredit you.

What's really exciting about this 'Do over' is, the fact that it's not a one-time thing. It's a daily thing. Every single day comes with new mercies. That simply means when you mess up and sin, don't try to hide it or excuse it. Confess it and work on it until you master it. I am faithful to extend to you brand new mercies so that you are forgiven, renewed, and without guilt or shame.

Here's a question for you: How far would you say the east is from the west? Not the east side of town from the west side, nor the east coast from the west coast, but in the stretch of eternity, how far is the east from the west? It's an impossible question to answer. It's the distance I have placed between you and your sins. Forget the past and all your past mistakes. The race is on, and the prize is before you. Keep your eye on the goal as you strive to secure the prize. You've got this!

POINTS TO PONDER: CAST INTO THE SEA

When we confess our sins, God casts them into the depths of the sea. The deepest sea is more than four miles deep; the distance of more than 84 football fields lined up end to end that separates us from our sins. Not only are they a tremendous distance from us, but God chooses to 'remember them no more'.

STUDY QUESTIONS

1. Think about a time when you were really sorry for something you had done and asked for forgiveness and the person said they forgave you, but they brought up the offense every opportunity they got. How does that make you feel?
2. When we are truly sorry and ask God for forgiveness, He forgives us, but sometimes we have trouble forgiving ourselves. What is the thing that you beat yourself up about, although God has forgiven you?
3. If we want forgiveness, we must learn to forgive others. No matter how horrible the offense is, God is willing and ready to forgive you when you confess it and sincerely ask for forgiveness. Describe the one offense you find most difficult to forgive and tell why.

DAY 28

When Life Gives You Crap

"For we are God's masterpiece. He has created us anew in Christ Jesus, so we can do the good things he planned for us long ago."

EPHESIANS 2:10 NLT

EVERYONE DISQUALIFIES YOU because of the very thing that qualifies you. They know of your struggles; they see the physical results of your emotional pain. They see your scars and think you're weak, but you're anything but weak.

They've heard your story, but not in its entirety. That's because it has not been completed yet. They've only had access to the first of its many chapters. What they don't realize is that you are a work of art in the making. You are God's workmanship, His work of art. (Everyone has an opinion about how you'll turn out based on what they've read so far.)

It may feel like everyone's placing bets against you. You hear things like, "she'll never amount to anything" or "she'll be just another teen statistic". You've got to remember that they're not the ones writing your story. That's God's job. They have no clue how bright your future is. All the crap that you've endured in the past is perfect fertilizer to produce the beautiful woman you are becoming, the beautiful woman that God has always intended you to be. The common crowd looks at your past and sees the crap, but the discerning few look beyond your past to see the beautiful blossom. When His healing work begins in you, you will begin to see yourself as He sees you. You are His beautiful masterpiece, undeniable by anyone who sees you.

POINTS TO PONDER: WHEN LIFE GIVES YOU CRAP

Think about your life as an unfinished book. All that you've endured in the past is history and cannot be changed, but, that chapter can be ended, and a new chapter can begin. Your past is just that- it has passed.

Your future is before you and the choices you make now will determine your tomorrows.

In the space below, name the chapters of your life/book: past, present, and future. Remember, you can't change your past, but you can shape your future.

The Life of ______________________________

Chapter 1: ______________________________

Chapter 2: ______________________________

Chapter 3: ______________________________

Chapter 4: ______________________________

Chapter 5: ______________________________

Chapter 6: ______________________________

Chapter 7: ______________________________

Chapter 8: ______________________________

Chapter 9: ______________________________

Chapter 10: ______________________________

DAY 29

From Pit to Palace

"The Lord is my helper, and I will not fear what man shall do unto me."

HEBREWS 13:6B KJV

JOSEPH WAS THE YOUNGEST OF 13 SIBLINGS and his father's favorite. As you can imagine, his brothers didn't like him much. To make matters worse, at 17 Joseph began having dreams. He dreamed that his brothers and even his father would bow down to him. They hated him even more.

Joseph's brothers plotted against him and threw him into a pit. They then devised a plot to kill him, telling their father that he had been eaten by a wild animal. Thankfully not all the brothers agreed to kill him, and so he was sold as a slave to passing merchants. The merchants then sold Joseph to Potiphar, who was a very high and powerful official in Egypt. Joseph became a common slave, but proved to be loyal to Potiphar, and, eventually, all of Egypt was placed under Joseph's charge.

Years later, there was a great famine in all the land, but because of Joseph's wisdom, Egypt had prepared for it. The only food to be bought or sold was in Egypt under his charge, and so Joseph's father sent his sons to Egypt to buy food. When Joseph saw his brothers, he recognized them at once, but they didn't recognize Joseph. The brothers bowed down to Joseph with their faces to the ground, in recognition of his position. Joseph eventually revealed himself to his brothers and they were terrified knowing what they had done. But Joseph consoled them saying, don't be angry with yourselves for throwing me into the pit and selling me as a slave. It was God's plan that I be placed here in a position to save your lives.

POINTS TO PONDER: FROM PIT TO PALACE

At 17, Joseph's life looked hopeless. The dream God had given him of others bowing down to him seemed impossible, but proved to be on point in the end. If you had met Joseph at the age of 17, you probably would have thought, 'what a mess'. How often do people judge us based on where we are right now? Joseph's story starts in a pit, but it ends in a palace. Had he not been thrown into the pit, he would not have made it to the palace. We all have pit experiences; the challenge is to make it a "pit stop" and not a lifelong dwelling place.

God used the pit experience to prepare Joseph for the palace promotion. We all have pit experiences, but how do we respond to them? We can't change the things that have happened, but we can learn from them and allow them to propel us into our destiny.

STUDY QUESTIONS

1. What have been some of your pit experiences?
2. How can God use your pit experiences to make your life better? Can others benefit from your pit experiences as well? How can you warn others of the pit just around the bend, so they don't fall in?
3. What are your aspirations in life? Are they a result of your pit experiences?

DAY 30

Who Are Your People?

"I will be a Father to you, and you will be my sons and daughters says the Lord Almighty."
2 CORINTHIANS 6:18 NIV

THERE'S 23AND ME, ANCESTRY DNA, and a host of other kits that can connect you to your past. It seems we are obsessed with knowing our lineage. I think secretly we hope to find that we're descendants of kings and queens. It makes for a nice fairytale, but it's not realistic. What if you had the chance to choose your ancestors? Would they be kings and queens?

Who do you think Jesus' ancestors were? There were a lot of them. But you'd probably never guess that right in the mix of all Jesus' ancestors are liars, adulterers, murderers, and a prostitute. Why would Jesus choose such a line up? Because he was in every way human, just as you and I are. He chose not to be born into royalty, but among the lowly. He shows us that none of us are beyond God's reach. He used a murderer as well as a prostitute. He used an unmarried teenage girl to fulfill the long awaited promise of a virgin's birth. Yes, Mary was just a teenage girl, who by saying yes to God gives birth to Jesus, the most influential person ever born, the Savior of the world. There is no doubt that He can and will use you if you say yes.

POINTS TO PONDER: WHO ARE YOUR PEOPLE?

As the saying goes, "you can't pick your family." I love my family, but some of my family members are pretty whacked. No matter how strange or dysfunctional your family is, they're yours. But when you accept Christ, you are adopted into the family of God. You gain a brand-new family and an inheritance beyond your comprehension.

STUDY QUESTIONS

1. Were you surprised to find that there were such 'shady' people in Jesus' family tree? What kind of people were you expecting to be there?
2. Why do you think Jesus would choose such ancestors? Who's the 'black sheep' in your family?
3. God's not looking for perfect people. He's looking for people who will say yes and become part of His family. Have you said yes to Him?

DAY 31

Casting Stones

"Do not judge, or you too will be judged."

MATTHEW 7:1 NIV

From the Father's Heart

OUT OF NOWHERE I'm brought this woman, obviously against her wishes. They were yelling and shouting that they'd caught her in the act of adultery. They were ready to stone her, and the law required it. The truth is, they were testing me. Would I set aside my teachings of compassion and uphold the law, having her put to death by stoning? Or would I ignore the prescribed law, and have compassion and show this woman mercy? Stoning the woman would contradict everything I've ever taught, and allowing the woman to go free would put me at odds with the law.

This incident happened long ago, but so little has changed. Adultery is not an act that can be committed alone, so where was the man? Why was he not judged? Was it simply because he was male, or perhaps his economic status got him off the hook? Whatever the reason, I scribbled in the sand, challenging those who brought her to me to consider their own lives. I won't tell you what was scribbled, only that it spoke to each individual. I further challenged those without sin to cast the first stone. No stones were cast that day.

Many have judged you, and you've placed value on their judgment based on your perception of them. Never measure your worth by the world's standards of superficial emptiness. When you're ready for a true assessment of who you are and your true worth, look to me. I've given my life for you, enduring the humiliating death by crucifixion. And that makes you worthy! The next time you're judged, give your accuser a stone, challenge them to throw only if their own life is perfect.

POINTS TO PONDER: CASTING STONES

There will always be people who are ready to judge you. Somehow, we feel elevated when we judge others, as if it makes us their superior. The woman who was brought to Jesus had committed a sin, and as it is stated, the punishment for that sin was death by stoning. Because of Jesus, the woman was not stoned. When we encounter Jesus, things change, but more importantly, we change.

STUDY QUESTIONS

1. Tell of a time when you unfairly judged someone based on their looks, race, or status.
2. Tell of a time when you were unfairly judged by others.
3. Tell of a time when you stood up for someone who was unfairly judged by others. How did it make you feel?

DAY 32

A Call for Justice

"But who so shall offend one of these little ones which believe in me, it were better for him that a millstone were hanged about his neck, and that he were drowned in the depth of the sea."

MATTHEWS 18:6 KJV

WHEN WE TALK ABOUT FORGIVENESS, we must understand that forgiveness is for the offended. It gives the offended freedom to move forward and seek healing. Forgiveness does not absolve the offense. The Bible tells us that offenses will come, but the offender should beware. It tells us that when a child is offended, it is better that a millstone be tied around his neck, and he be thrown into the sea. That millstone would be like having a concrete wheel tied to the predator, and then throwing him into the depths of the sea. God recognizes the need for justice.

Revenge and justice are two completely different things, with completely different motives. Revenge's motive is to get even; it's the 'an eye for an eye attitude'. Rather than bringing closure to the situation, it has the potential to become a never-ending cycle. Justice is the result of due process of the law. Its motive is to seek truth and execute fair and just punishment. Justice brings closure and accelerates healing.

When justice is not possible, we can find solace in the fact that nothing escapes the eyes of God. This is not karma. It's a biblical principle, 'whatever you sow, that you will also reap!'

POINTS TO PONDER: A CALL FOR JUSTICE

Children are gifts from God, they are innocent and the most vulnerable among us. God has placed the charge of children in the hands of adults who would love, provide, protect, discipline and sacrifice for them. They are our greatest gifts and deserve strong justice.

STUDY QUESTIONS

1. Have you been seeking justice or revenge for the person who offended you?
2. It's flawed to think that forgiveness negates justice. What do you see as fair and just punishment for your perpetrator?
3. If your perpetrator is never brought to justice, can you find solace in the fact that God sees all and He will ultimately execute judgement?

DAY 33

Grenade?

"Greater love hath no man than this, that a man lay down his life for his friends."

JOHN 15:13 KJV

YOU KNOW THAT FRIEND YOU HAVE whose life seems to be perfect? But then when you see their number on the phone, you think, 'what could they want now? The truth is the only time you hear from them is when they need something, the notes from history class, a mutual friend's cell number, something. Because it's the only time you hear from them. Maybe you should change their title from friend to dependent, since they're always depending on you for something.

Be careful not to treat God that way, only showing up when you're in need of something. He'd love to hear from you when you're not in need. He wants a very personal intimate relationship, one where you would seek His counsel and He would direct your steps. Don't treat God like He's your personal genie ready to grant your every wish, or your personal Bail Bondsman, ready to bail you out of every sticky mess you get yourself into. It gives Him pleasure to give His children the things they need and want.

In Bruno Mars' hit song, *Grenade,* he says he'll "catch a grenade for you, throw his hand on a blade for you, jump in front of a train for you." He says he'll do anything for you, even take a bullet through the brain for you. Well don't count on it. What you can count on is God wanting a relationship with you so much that He allowed His son Jesus to suffer death by crucifixion for you.

POINTS TO PONDER: GRENADE?

When was the last time you spoke to God? You know, prayed? Was it like a long Amazon order, listing all the things you want? Or was it like a long appeal to Santa Clause, trying to convince him you've been good and deserving? Do you thank God for what He has already provided?

Unlike the empty promises of those declaring that they'd take a bullet for you, He's already given His son for you. God wants us to ask for what we need, but we should first recognize and be thankful for what He's already provided.

STUDY QUESTIONS

1. Have you treated God like your personal genie, promising never to do again the thing that has gotten you into trouble? Think back on the last mess you got yourself into. Things could have gone quite differently. Now would be a good time to say, 'thank you, God'.
2. God is faithful to you even when you are not faithful to Him. In spite of your actions God has given His son to take your place and pay for the sins, that you committed. And He continues to love and pursue you. Aren't you glad that God is not like us? In 3-5 sentences describe how you see God's faithfulness in your life.
3. Praying can be difficult if you don't have a relationship with God. To develop a relationship, grab a notebook and start a gratitude journal. Each morning list 3 things you are thankful for, start in the space below.

    1. ____

    2. ____

    3: ____

DAY 34

My Prodigal Daughter

*"For this (daughter) of mine was dead and is alive again;
(she) was lost and is found.' So they began to celebrate."*

LUKE 15:24 NIV

From the Father's Heart

IT'S TRUE THAT even before the earth was formed, I knew everything about you. And I knew the very day that you would run. Still when that day came, I was heartbroken. I have given you free will, so that you can freely choose your path in life, even knowing that you may not choose me. The other option would have been to create a mindless soul, blindly marching to my beat, the beat of your creator. I created you with purpose, and with a mind and will of your own, so the choice is always yours, even when it's not me that you choose.

The day you ran for the first time, my heart broke, because I could clearly see what awaited you. That first time and each time since, I have relentlessly pursued you, wooing you back to me. Many times, I've pulled you back from seen and unseen dangers to keep you safe. Now I sit here waiting for your return, peering into the distance with the finest robe designed especially for you, a robe of righteousness. And when I see you, even from a distance, I will know you and I will put aside my status, and I will run to you. I will greet you with a holy embrace, covering you with the robe. I will place shoes on your feet, shoes that will take you in a new direction, and a ring on your finger, signifying that you are mine. For you, my prodigal daughter who was once lost will have been found, and I and all of heaven will rejoice.

POINTS TO PONDER: MY PRODIGAL DAUGHTER

I want you to know the love that I have for you. I want you to know that I still sit and wait for your return, holding your beautiful white robe.

I sit ready to run at any time to meet you and embrace you and rejoice with all of heaven. Please come home!

STUDY QUESTIONS

1. God has given you free will, and that free will has gotten you into some dangerous situations. Why do you think God who has the ability to make us obedient, gives us free will, knowing what a mess we will make?
2. The Father wants to place new shoes on your feet that will take you in a new direction. Describe the old direction you've been walking in and its consequences and pitfalls.
3. The ring the Father will place on your finger is not just any ring, but a signet ring. It designates authority and honor. Earnestly and tenderly Jesus softly calls to you to come home. Why have you not answered the call?

DAY 35

What's Your Issue?

"Daughter, your faith has healed you. Go in peace."

LUKE 8:48 NIV

CAN YOU IMAGINE NOT BEING ACCEPTED by people because you're on your period? Well, that's the way it was in biblical days. On one occasion when Jesus was teaching a large crowd of people there was a woman in the crowd who was sick. She had been bleeding for 12 years. She had gone to many doctors, but none could help her. She had heard about Jesus, but the law said she couldn't be around others because of her bleeding.

This woman was so convinced that Jesus was the answer to her problem, that she decided to go to Him, despite the law. She had this tremendous faith that Jesus could heal her, even though none of the doctors could. This woman's name is never given; she's only known by her condition.

During the 12 years she had the condition, everyone had probably given up on her, including her family and friends. So often you are known by your condition or the trauma you've endured, especially when you've suffered for years. You must not believe the lie that you'll just have to learn to live with it. Even though the woman's condition made her an outcast, her determination made her push pass the crowd to reach Jesus. She hadn't planned to say anything. She was desperate for God. Her one thought was, "If I could just get close enough to touch the hem of his clothing, I will be healed."

When you are desperate for God, you'll stop caring about the opinions of your family, friends, and others. When you are desperate enough, you'll forget about everyone around you, and you'll push past all your anxieties and doubts, and reach out to God. Just as the woman in the story found healing, you'll find God waiting and ready to meet your needs.

POINTS TO PONDER: WHAT'S YOUR ISSUE?

Like the woman in the story, people may label you by what you've suffered, rather than who you really are, but you don't have to accept their labels. You don't have to answer to what they call you. You've already learned some of the things God says about you, and they're all positive things. God wants to heal you from your past experiences. His hand is already extended, reach out and grab it.

STUDY QUESTIONS

1. What are you suffering from, physically, spiritually or emotionally?
2. Do you feel like people know you only by what you've experienced, rather than who you are? If so, how does that make you feel?
3. Are you desperate enough to reach out to Jesus for your healing? If not, what would it take to get you there?

DAY 36

A New You

"This means that anyone who belongs to Christ has become a new person. The old life is gone; a new life has begun!"
2 CORINTHIANS 5:17 NLT

From the Father's Heart

EVERYTHING ABOUT YOU reminds me of Saul. Saul is someone I knew a long time ago. He was a man to be admired, a man of passion. Saul promoted what he believed in such a way that if you met him, he'd enthusiastically share his beliefs with you and condemn anything contrary to what he believed. The problem: Saul had a false belief system.

I love your passion. When you commit to something, you are truly committed. I'm impressed with the level of fight you expend to get what you want. You will argue your point for hours without fail. It's the thing I really love about you, but like Saul, you're very often wrong. Saul was so committed to his beliefs, that it took a supernatural encounter for him to see the light.

Saul's heart was hard; he passionately spoke against my teachings. I changed the heart of Saul and caused him to see the light. Once he recognized the truth, he made a drastic change. With the same passion and enthusiasm he spoke against my teachings, once seeing the light, he began to teach and even preach the Truth. The change was so drastic that I even changed his name. Instead of Saul, he became Paul. I won't change your name. But if you allow me to, I will change you in such a way that everyone will see the new and improved you and be astonished.

POINTS TO PONDER: A NEW YOU

I think I've got your attention, so I'm sending those who can help you see the light. I'd love to speak directly to you, but you haven't learned to recognize my voice yet. That will come, but for now hear what I have to say to you through others.

STUDY QUESTIONS

1. What are your passions, and how do they affect the people around you?
2. What would your life look like if you had the same type of experience Paul had, going from being totally against Christians and Jesus to being a total believer teaching and preaching the Gospel?
3. Much of your life has been lived in darkness. Would you be willing to hear a different perspective and have that darkness turned to light?

DAY 37

All the King's Horses

"Though he fall, he shall not be utterly cast down: for the Lord upholdeth him with his hand."

PSALMS 37:24 KJV

HUMPTY DUMPTY SAT ON THE WALL. Humpty Dumpty had a great fall. Imagine seeing yourself in a child's nursery rhyme. There's no denying it, for we can all be seen as Humpty Dumpty at one time or another. It's clear that Humpty's a fragile egg, but he was still able to maintain his world, comfortably on his wall.

I'm always curiously wondering what caused the fall. Every illustration shows Humpty securely sitting on the wall and then 'splat', out of nowhere he's on the ground. Could it be the ups and downs of life that caused Humpty to fall? Was it a great Northern wind that blew up causing the tumble? Or perhaps something more sinister, like suffering abuse at the hands of others? Perhaps it was no fall at all, perhaps Humpty was pushed. We're not given the privilege of knowing what caused the fall, however, the results are the same: Humpty falls to pieces.

How many times have you fallen to pieces because of a fall or, maybe, a push? There are some falls we can recover from rather quickly. We can get up, shake ourselves, attend to our scrapes and bruises, push our pride and embarrassment aside, and get back on the wall.

There are other times when the damage is too great. Like Humpty, we find ourselves broken far beyond our own ability to repair. The recovery requires the help of others. Humpty recognized that and sought outside help. Humpty sought help from all the king's horses and all the king's men, but none were able to put him together again.

How unfortunate that Humpty would seek help from the king's horses and the king's men, but not from the King himself. How often do we in our broken state seek help from others who are broken? Sometimes we're not seeking the help of a person, but a vice. Be it bottle, bong, cutting or a host of other temporary fixes, in the end the problem returns with a vengeance. How often do we overlook the true source of help, from the one who has come to restore us to our former glory? The source of our true healing comes from the King of Kings! He is the only one who is able to make us new again.

POINTS TO PONDER: ALL THE KING'S HORSES

Life can be brutal! There are so many things beyond our control that can break us. Then, after we lay shattered to pieces, naysayers gather to look, as if we're on display for their critique. How do you respond when others have fallen? Let's not kick them when they're down. Instead, let's offer them a hand up.

STUDY QUESTIONS

1. Many adopt unhealthy habits in an attempt to 'fix' themselves. What have you used to try to fix yourself or to numb the pain of brokenness?
2. Who or what do you turn to when your life is falling apart and you can't seem to put the pieces back together? Has that worked for you in the past?
3. Jesus can put your brokenness back together again, but it requires that you trust Him. Are you willing to trust Him with your brokenness?

DAY 38

Battle Scars

"But he said to me, "My grace is sufficient for you, for my power is made perfect in weakness." Therefore, I will boast all the more gladly about my weaknesses, so that Christ's power may rest on me. That is why, for Christ's sake, I delight in weaknesses, in insults, in hardships, in persecutions, in difficulties. For when I am weak, then I am strong."

2 CORINTHIANS 12:9-10 NIV

From the Father's Heart

PAUL IS A GREAT FIGURE in the Bible. He wrote most of the New Testament, and I used him to do great things. But Paul wasn't without problems, he lived with a condition that was very uncomfortable. He referred to it as 'a thorn in his flesh'. Three times Paul asked to be healed, but the answer was 'no'. Instead his condition was used to show others the power of faith in me, the true and living God.

As hard as your past has been, don't despise it, use it. When your battle scars are fully healed, share your story. Tell it to others who are facing some of the same challenges. Be like the old veteran who proudly exposes his chest, revealing the scars he received while defending his country. Tell others how you tried numbing the pain with alcohol and drugs, but the pain, like a homing pigeon, would always find its way back to you. Tell them how you sought peace in a pipe, rather than in me, the Prince of Peace. Roll up your sleeves, show them the marks where you've cut, choosing to feel physical pain rather than the unbearable emotional pain.

Bear your battle scars proudly. Sure, you've been knocked down, but never knocked out. You've lost some battles, but you've stayed in the fight and ultimately you win the war. I too bear battle scars. You'll have a chance to examine the nail prints in my hands and in my feet. I proudly wear them. It's by those scars that I was able to save the world. Your scars too, will be the antidote that will bring healing. Don't allow your pride to be an obstacle!

POINTS TO PONDER: BATTLE SCARS

"Into each life some rain must fall" or "everybody gets crap to deal with." No matter how you look at it, we all have battle scars. When you think about it, God allowed His only son to suffer at the hands of evil men, so in a very real way, Jesus identifies with those who suffer at the hands of others.

STUDY QUESTIONS

1. What vices have you used to numb the pain of your past?
2. What appropriate coping skills have you learned and are using?
3. Paul wrote two thirds of the New Testament and shared the gospel with countless numbers of people in spite of his condition. He used the weakness of his condition to point others to his strength that came from his relationship with Jesus. How can you use your past to point others to Jesus?
4. What does the last line of day thirty-eight mean to you? How can your pride be an obstacle in the healing of others?

DAY 39

I Have Redeemed You

"Fear not, for I have redeemed you; I have called you by name, you are mine..."

ISAIAH 43:1C NKJV

From the Father's Heart

THERE IS NO NEED TO BE AFRAID, I have called you by your name, you are mine. When I look deep into your eyes and even deeper into your heart, I see a reflection of myself. I see the you that others don't see, can't see, or refuse to see. I created you in my own image. You are mine, and when you were taken from me, I paid the ransom. No cost was too great, not even my life. You are my beloved. I am fully invested in you, and I will allow nothing to overtake you. Be it flood or fire you will not drown, nor will you be burned.

I have known you before time existed, and in every possible way. I know your innermost parts and your most intimate thoughts. I've collected your tears in a bottle, and there have been many. I've placed your prayers in a bowl. I know each hair on your head. I know your thoughts before you think them. Still, you've not learned to fully trust me, but you must trust that no matter what happens in your life, I will never leave you or forsake you.

Be determined to know me in ways most people don't. Read what I've written and know the thoughts I have toward you. Examine my wounds and know that, like you, I too have suffered. Know that there is nothing that you have suffered or will suffer, that I have not suffered before you.

There are those who seek to harm you, wishing to pick you to pieces, but I have prayed for you, and when your time has come, your faith will not fail. Then we will not only walk together, but also work together. You will be my mouthpiece, strengthening others, and showing them the way to new life.

POINTS TO PONDER: I HAVE REDEEMED YOU

What a great feeling to know that God knows my name, and says to me, don't be afraid. When He tells me that I belong to Him, there is no better feeling. God wants to have that same relationship with you. God wants to use you in sharing your story to help others avoid some of the pitfalls you've had. Saying yes to God is saying yes to your purpose in life.

STUDY QUESTIONS

1. How do you feel knowing God knows your thoughts, even before you think them?
2. In what ways do you think God could use your story to help others heal?
3. Can you imagine yourself speaking for God by sharing His love with others?

DAY 40

The Company We Keep

"Don't you realize that those who do wrong will not inherit the Kingdom of God? ... Some of you were once like that. But you were cleansed; you were made holy; you were made right with God by calling on the name of the Lord Jesus Christ and by the Spirit of our God."

1 CORINTHIANS 6:9a,11 NLT

IF THE PRESIDENT OF THE UNITED STATES were visiting your city it's not likely that he would stay at your house. It's more likely that he'd stay at the ritziest place in town. So what about Jesus? Where do you think Jesus would stay? He'd stay at my house or yours. That's how Jesus rolled. He'd decline hanging out with the 'rich and famous,' to hang out with you and me, the 'ordinary people'.

Jesus was pretty cool. Just think about it. He's God's son. He could have hung out with the equivalent of the Pope at that time but He chose to hang out with sinners and tax collectors. Tax collectors were hated by everybody, because they were thieves. They would collect taxes from the poor to give to the rich, and they'd always collect a little extra for themselves. Jesus was judged for hanging out with them, but He didn't let that stop Him.

Grab your Bible. Let's take a look at one of the many people Jesus hung out with: Read John 4:1-30. You'll find Jesus hanging out with a Samaritan woman. A Jew and a Samaritan hanging out would be the equivalent of a Black and White hanging out in the 1950's. It was unheard of. In hearing their conversation, you find out that this woman had quite a past. Not even Jesus' disciples approved, but that conversation, that day at the well, changed that woman's life forever. When you have a real encounter with Jesus, you too will have a forever changed life.

POINTS TO PONDER: THE COMPANY WE KEEP

A couple I know went on vacation to Puerto Rico. They didn't know anyone in Puerto Rico, so they checked on line and saw the beautiful beaches with its sparkling waters. They stayed at a beautiful five-star hotel and the beaches were pristine. It was all they anticipated.

Then they had this idea to leave the commercial tourist areas and check out the lives of everyday citizens. It was then they learned that the people were poor, and crime was high. Their lives were not highlighted in the brochures. That's the reason Jesus would choose to stay at your house or mine, rather than with the 'rich and famous'. He identifies with us. Unlike my friends, He doesn't come to kick back and have a lovely vacation. He comes to bring about change. When you invite Jesus into your heart, to stay at your house, like the woman at the well, you'll never be the same.

STUDY QUESTIONS

1. If Jesus were to come and stay at your house, what things would you have to get rid of? Who are the people you'd ask to leave before He arrives?
2. Who are the people you would insist on coming over to meet Jesus?
3. If given the opportunity to ask Jesus only three questions, what would they be?

    1. ____
    2. ____
    3. ____

FINAL BONUS

Who is this Jesus?

"Jesus saith unto him, 'I am the way, the truth, and the life: no man cometh unto the Father, but by me.'"

JOHN 14:6 KJV

IF I COULD ARRANGE MY OWN BIRTH, it would be quite spectacular. My parents would be rich beyond measure, and I would have everything I could ever want.

But what about Jesus? He had the ability to arrange his own birth, but rather than a palace, he was born in a stable. Take a good look at Jesus: Don't be fooled by the pictures you see. He was not handsome or majestic in appearance, there was nothing that would attract you to him. He was despised and rejected by mankind. He knew suffering and pain. You wouldn't have given him a second look; he was despised and rejected. You would have counted Him as being beneath you.

The truth is, the pain he endured was for you. He took all your sin, every wrong thing that you have ever done and every wrong thing that you will ever do. Jesus took on the consequence of your sin, and sin always has its consequences. The consequence of your sin was death by crucifixion! So, for you and me, Jesus was nailed to a cross.

The next time you see a portrait of Jesus with his neatly trimmed beard, his beautiful blue eyes, his shoulder length well-groomed hair and his flawless complexion, think of it as an Instagram or snapchat pic with a filter, making the not so attractive look attractive. A more accurate picture might be an average looking rugged guy, whose body shows the signs of suffering and pain, and yet his eyes would show the extraordinary depth of his love for you.

FINAL BONUS: THE BIG DECISION

The purpose of *War Dancer* is that you get to know Jesus. It may be that He's not who you thought He was. He's not distant and aloof, He is as close as the air you breath. He's been tugging at your heart trying to get your attention, but you've been so caught up in your daily empty routine that you've not felt the tugging, nor have you heard the messages He's sent.

Will you make today your day of decision? Will you make today the day you say "YES'? Consider everything that you've learned about God the Father, Jesus the Son, and His Spirit, that wants to live in you and remind you of all the wonderful things you've read and learned these past 40 days.

Jesus died a very painful death on the cross for all of us. He's given His life for every person that's ever lived. Millions have said yes to the forgiveness of sin that He offers, and millions have refused His offer. Yet He continues to love and pursue even those who reject Him. What is your decision? Are you saying 'yes' to the love of the Father? Are you saying 'yes' to Jesus and the forgiveness of sins that He freely gives? Are you saying yes to the Spirit living in you, to guide you, and lead you, and remind you of all you have learned? Today is the day of salvation, choose wisely, say 'yes' today.

The next few pages will tell you step by step how to say "yes" to the most important decision you'll ever make, not only in this life but the after-life as well. If you've already said yes, use this as a time to recommit your life and devotion to Christ.

The Roman Road

ALL HAVE SINNED – ROMANS 3:10,23

That means everyone: you have sinned, I have sinned, your precious granny has sinned. Sin is what separates us from God.

THE PUNISHMENT FOR SIN IS DEATH – ROMANS 6:23

Sin has its price. It's a costly price that comes with the sentencing of death.

JESUS PAID OUR SIN DEBT – ROMANS 5:8

Our debt had to be paid, and because God's love for us is so great, he sent his own son, Jesus, who had no sin, to pay our sin debt by dying on Calvary's cross in our place.

SALVATION COMES BY FAITH – ROMANS 10:9,10

If we confess with our mouth that Jesus is Lord, and believe in our heart that God raised Jesus from the dead, we shall be saved.

In essence, Jesus became our substitute by living the perfect life that we could not live. He then died the death that we deserved to die. When He was raised from the dead, we were raised with Him, to a new life in Him.

If you believe and trust in Jesus and what he's done for you, pray the prayer on the next page and welcome to the Body of Christ.

Prayer of Decision

Hi God,

It's me ________________________________

For the first time I feel like someone really gets me. People think that I'm happy, fun and carefree, but the truth is, I have always felt so empty. No matter what I do or who I'm with, it's never enough. I always feel like something is missing. I never fully understood, but now I know that it was you! You are what's missing in my life.

On today, ________________________________

I'm saying yes! Yes, I want a personal relationship with you. No, I don't understand all that it means, but I'm trusting you. I can't imagine that a perfect and Holy God wants to have a relationship with a very imperfect person with so many problems like me, but I want what you're offering. I want everything you're offering.

I accept your gift of life. I accept the gift of your son Jesus, who died for me a sinner. I accept that He paid for all the sins that I have committed and will commit. I will continue looking to Him for grace, forgiveness and love. Thank you for wiping my slate clean and giving me a brand-new start.

Amen

In the prayer above fill in your name and the date of decision.

What Now?

WELCOME TO THE FAMILY. You are born again and are now a part of the Family of God. That means you have a kinship with believers all over the world who have taken the same steps you have and accepted Christ. So, what now?

Right now you are a baby in the family, and like a baby there is lots to learn. First, find a Bible believing church that has an active youth ministry to help you learn and grow. If you don't have a Bible already, get one. Look for one that is easy to read and geared to young people.

Faith is the key to your new life in Christ. Romans 10:17 tells us that faith comes by hearing the word of God. That's why it's so important that we read our Bibles, so we can increase our faith. One of God's many special gifts to you is the gift of the Holy Spirit, God's own personal presence in you, to guide you and teach you through His word, the Bible.

Another part of your new life is prayer. Prayer is like a private connection to God. It can be hard getting started, but soon you'll find your days go so much better when you start with prayer.

The real key to your new life in Christ is staying connected to a Bible believing/teaching church. Get involved in a youth group and find friends who are also in the family of God. Although your life won't be problem free, you'll find the problems much easier to bear.

A Final Word

If this devotional has helped you in any way, drop us a line. We'd love to hear from you.

Life Restored SA
Attn: War Dancer
14546 Brook Hollow #405
San Antonio, TX 78232

www.liferestoredsa.org

Acknowledgements

The telltale sign that I am one of God's favorite people is the reality that He has lavished me with such wonderful friends, and a ministry team that is totally committed to Him. I am forever grateful for what appeared to be a random coming together of those with a heart for ministry. I now recognize the precision in which God has knitted our hearts together for such a time as this. A time in history where sexual assault is on the rise and sex trafficking is the fastest growing crime in the world. Mary Williams, my personal prayer warrior, was the continual reminder that writing this book was the call of God on my life. Sara Ames would softly whisper encouragement, trusting that God's conviction would get the book to its completion. Sherry Thompson and Jill Powell, would show up periodically, keeping me steadfast in my pursuit to bring this book to its completion.

In addition, I am forever grateful for my "Believers I Am" Bible study group of New Creation Christian Fellowship, who unknowingly kept me encouraged, challenging me to fulfill my God given purpose. Declaring that there was a book within me that needed to be birthed.

Lastly, but certainly not least I must acknowledge the beautiful, sweet girls who are survivors of sex trafficking. Thank you for allowing me to walk alongside you and point you to Jesus, the ultimate healer who brings complete restoration. You have given me purpose. You have been the catalyst that has shoved me into the arms of God. I love each of you.

About the Author

I grew up in a relatively safe time and in a very safe environment. It's what I wanted for my girls. I raised them as I was brought up, with a strong Christian background. Nevertheless, my youngest daughter was trafficked at the age of 14. I was blindsided!

My daughter endured the ultimate abuse of being bought and sold. The abuse was not only sexual, but emotional, mental, physical, and even spiritual. At that time, we didn't know what we know today about the complex trauma of Domestic Minor Sex Trafficking (DMST).

My daughter unfortunately took on the shame of what happened to her. Shame is born out of humiliation for wrong or foolish behavior and was clearly not hers to bear. However, due to the mental abuse she endured, she believed the situation was her fault. She assumed the responsibility for the abuse and trauma she experienced which compounded the trauma. Children are never responsible for the actions of adults!

As a mother and a woman of faith, I sought God, and He began to give me insight on the depth of pain and hurt my daughter and so many of His precious young people have endured. *War Dancer* is the result of God's insight and heart for all who have experienced the pain and suffering of this horrific abuse. My hope and prayer for this 40 day devotional is that every person, young or old, would come to realize that they are loved by the Father, and that they are worthy!

About Life Restored of San Antonio

Life Restored SA (LRSA) is a faith based, God breathed, non-profit organization, birthed out of the pain of my 14-year-old daughter being trafficked. The mission of LRSA is to restore hope and purpose to exploited youth and their families by offering emotional, physical and spiritual healing. Our ultimate goal is seeing their lives redeemed through a personal relationship with Jesus Christ.

Domestic Minor Sex Trafficking (DMST), that is selling children under the age of 18, is the fastest growing crime in the world. In addition to sounding the alarm and bringing awareness to this, we walk alongside the survivors and lead them to the Healer. The content of *War Dancer* is one of the many tools God continues to use in ministering to those we serve. Our goal is to put a copy in the hands of every girl and young woman that comes through this ministry.

Your tax deductible support of this ministry is greatly appreciated. In fact, because we are determined to be fully faith based and God inspired, we depend on the financial support of Churches and individuals like yourself. God has given LRSA a heart for those who are 'the least of these', to sow into this ministry is to share in the harvest that is reaped.

Visit our website at **www.liferestoredsa.org** and join the fight against sexual exploitation by becoming a Traffic Jammer today.